Walking
KYOTO

古 都 千 年 の 彩 譜

辻本洋太朗 絵・文
コルーチィ・ステラ 訳

A Thousand Years of Splendor

Walking KYOTO
A Thousand Years of Splendor

Published and distributed by
MAMUKAI Books Gallery

3-14-19-6F Shibaura, Minato-ku, Tokyo 108-0023
+81 (50) 3555 7335
www.mamukai.com

Editors:	Yukako Kimura, Takashi Kanazawa
Designer:	Atsuko Kabeyasawa
Digital Director:	SEKINE Advertising
Special thanks to:	Michiyo Yamamoto

ISBN 978-4-904402-05-4
Cataloging in publication data: National Diet Library, Japan

Illustrations and text copyright ©2016 by Yohtaro Tsujimoto
Translation copyright ©2016 by Stella Colucci
All rights reserved.

Printed in Japan

2 3 4 5 6 7 8 9 10

FROM THE TRANSLATOR

In this book, the author has written anecdotes to his sketches as an introduction to interesting stories you might enjoy from further reading. The names of historical characters and famous individuals are listed in the Japanese order of last name-first name. The author has also included information to help you explore areas around the places included in this collection. Access information is provided for your convenience, but please note that there may be several ways to reach your destination. To find your best way, please consult maps and travel guides.

FOREWORD

Kyoto, the ancient capital of a millenium, is a city with deep secrets in history, the different periods layering themselves upon one another. It is fascinating to imagine the characters who influenced the times. The people of Kyoto have weathered natural disasters, disease and conflicts, rebuilding after each tragic event. Their music, tradional culture, literature, crafts, art and cuisine are very deep-rooted in daily life. Behind each of my simple sketches is a story. If you were to get to know even a small part of that story, these sketches might become more interesting. Although this book introduces you to just a glimpse of Kyoto, I do hope you enjoy exploring these pages.

Yohtaro Tsujimoto

はじめに

　千年の古都・京都は濃密に史跡が残る街。幾層にも時代の歴史が積み重なってきた。その時代に活躍した人物を想像するのも楽しい。そして天災、疫病、戦乱など悲惨な嵐を人々は耐え、再生を繰り返してきた。その生活の中に歌舞音曲、茶花、文学、絵画工芸そして優雅な京料理が庶民の中にも浸透している。

　このシンプルな風景スケッチにもそれぞれの背景がある。それを少し知るだけでスケッチの楽しみ、喜びは増幅する。京都のほんの一部の紹介にしか過ぎませんが、誌上散策をお楽しみください。

辻本洋太朗

CONTENTS 目次

Foreword　はじめに ………… 3

Collection: **Seasons**　特集 京の四季 ………… 6
Collection: **Nature**　特集 京の自然 ………… 8

洛中 Kyoto Central

Kyoto Imperial Palace and Mt.Daimonji　京都御苑と大文字山 ………… 10
Shokoku-ji Temple　相国寺 ………… 11
Takasegawa Ichi-no-funairi　高瀬川一之船入 ………… 12
Kamogawa and Noryo-yuka　鴨川と納涼床 ………… 13
Ponto-cho　先斗町 ………… 14
Kyoto Nishiki Food Market　錦市場 ………… 15
Nijo-jo Castle Higashi Otemon Gate　二条城・東大手門 ………… 16
Kitano Tenmangu Shrine　北野天満宮 ………… 17
Daitoku-ji Temple　大徳寺 芳春院への小径 ………… 18
Kinkaku-ji Temple (The Golden Pavilion)　金閣寺 ………… 19
Myoshin-ji Temple　妙心寺 ………… 20
Ninna-ji Temple　仁和寺 ………… 21
Higashi Hongan-ji Temple　東本願寺 ………… 22
To-ji Temple　東寺 ………… 23

洛東 Kyoto East

Tofuku-ji Temple　東福寺・通天橋 ………… 24
Kiyomizu-dera Temple　清水寺 ………… 25
Sannenzaka　三年坂 ………… 26
Yasaka Pagoda　八坂の塔 ………… 27
Nene-no-Michi　ねゝの道 ………… 28
Kyoto Minamiza Theatre　南座・顔見世興行 ………… 29
Gion Shinbashi　祇園新橋の桜 ………… 30
Chion-in Temple　知恩院 ………… 31
Nanzen-ji Temple　南禅寺 ………… 32
Honen-in Temple　法然院 ………… 33
Ginkaku-ji Temple (The Silver Pavilion)　銀閣寺 ………… 34

洛北 Kyoto North

Mt. Hiei　植物園から望む比叡山 ···················· 36
Shake-machi　社家町 ···················· 37
Sanzen-in Temple　大原三千院・往生極楽院 ···················· 38
Ohara in Autumn　大原の秋 ···················· 39
Jakko-in Temple　雪の寂光院 ···················· 40
Kitayama Cedars　北山杉の郷 ···················· 41

洛西 Kyoto West

Tenryu-ji Temple　天龍寺 ···················· 44
Togetsu-kyo Bridge　嵐山渡月橋 ···················· 45
Saga Bamboo Forest　嵯峨竹林 ···················· 46
Gio-ji Temple　祇王寺 ···················· 47
Rakushisha　落柿舎 ···················· 48
Adashino Nenbutsu-ji Temple　化野念仏寺 ···················· 49
Saga Toriimoto　嵯峨鳥居本 ···················· 50
Sagano in Spring　嵯峨野の春 ···················· 51
Daikaku-ji Temple Osawa Pond　大覚寺・大沢池 ···················· 52
Jingo-ji Temple　神護寺 ···················· 53
Hozu River boat ride　保津川下り ···················· 54
Katsura Imperial Villa　桂離宮 ···················· 55

洛南 Kyoto South

Fushimi Inari-taisha Shrine　伏見稲荷神社参道 ···················· 56
Canal Along Fushimi Sake District　伏見酒蔵と運河 ···················· 57
Daigo-ji Temple　醍醐寺・桜の馬場 ···················· 58
Byodo-in Temple　平等院 ···················· 59
Tea Fields of Uji　宇治茶の郷 ···················· 60

コラム Features

Around town　京の町角 ···················· 35
At the temples　京の庭園・仏像 ···················· 42
Festivals　京の祭 ···················· 43
Culture　京の雅 ···················· 61

Walking KYOTO map ···················· 62
More information　英訳追記 ···················· 63
Cutouts and postcards ···················· 67

Collection: **Seasons**　特集 京の四季

春 Spring　　Spring at Kiyomizu Temple　清水寺の春　　東山区・清水

夏 Summer　　Gion Festival Float (*naginata hoko*)　祇園祭 長刀鉾の辻廻し　　中京区・御池通

秋 Autumn　Atagoyama Ichi no Torii　愛宕山一之鳥居　右京区・嵯峨鳥居本

冬 Winter　Winter migrators (*miyako dori*)　都鳥　中京区・三条大橋

Collection: **Nature**　特集 京の自然

Sagano and Hirosawa Pond
嵯峨野と広沢池　右京区・嵯峨広沢

Hozu River boat ride
保津川下り
右京区・嵯峨水尾

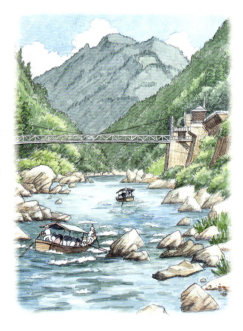

Autumn, satoyama
里山の秋　左京区・大原

Kamo Ohashi
賀茂大橋
左京区・下鴨

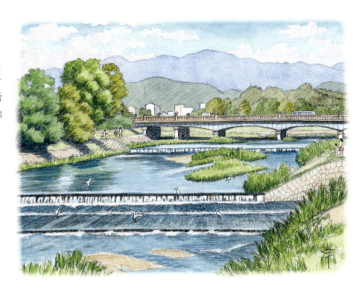

Hieizan colored in autumn
比叡山黄葉
左京区・山端

Jizo-do under snow
雪の地蔵堂
南丹市・美山北

洛中 Kyoto Central

Kyoto Imperial Palace and Mt. Daimonji

The Greater Imperial Palace was originally about 1.5 km west of the current location. Heian-kyo, established in 794 AD, declined as devastation spread from Kyoto West, and the Palace was repeatedly engulfed in flames. Court was moved often and held in the villas of aristocrats before finally settling in the present location. More than half of Kyoto Central burned down during skirmishes that led to the end of the Edo Period. The Palace was left in ruins, but the former villas have since been restored as Kyoto Gyoen (see P63). On Mt. Daimonji to the east, flaming torches create a spectacular view on a dark summer night as part of *Gozan no Okuribi*. To the north are Shokoku-ji and Doshisha University; the Kamo River flows to the east. Shop for souvenirs around the Palace in the stores of former purveyors to the Imperial Household.

京都御苑と大文字山　　　　　　　　　　　　　　　　　　　　　　上京区・京都御苑

　現在の御所から西へ1.5km、千本丸太町近くの公園に「大極殿遺趾」の石碑が建つ。平安京（794年）は西から荒廃、内裏は幾度も焼失した。朝廷は公家の屋敷を借りる里内裏の時代が続き、現在地に落ち着いた。武家の時代には実権もなくなり、公家達は内裏の周囲に居を構えた。幕末には風雲急を告げる舞台となり、「蛤御門の変」では洛中の半分が焼失。東京遷都で御所は荒廃したが、公家達の屋敷跡は整備されて京都御苑となった。東に見える大文字は五山の送り火。夏の闇夜に燃え上がる大文字は幻想的だ。御苑のすぐ北には相国寺、同志社大学。東には鴨川が流れる。御所の周囲には朝廷御用達の老舗が多かった。風格のある老舗で食品、伝統工芸品を求めて散策するのも楽しい。

Shokoku-ji Temple

The seat of government that had moved to Kamakura for 150 years returned to Kyoto in 1336. Yoshimitsu, the third Ashikaga shogun, resided in Muromachi opulence at the Palace of Flowers and built the expansive Shokoku-ji Temple next door. The 109 m tall seven-story pagoda has since been lost to a lightning strike. Known as "the chanting temple" (*shomyo zura*) because voices are amplified as monks chant the sutra, this Zen temple was a gathering place for elite priests who excelled in academics, calligraphy and literature; among them, master artists Jakuchu, Shubun and Sesshu. In Demachi, where the Kamo and Takano Rivers meet east of Shokokuji, the Shimogamo Shrine is a World Heritage site famous for horseback archery exhibitions during the Aoi Festival. The surrounding Tadasu Forest has preserved the pure landscape over time, as if to wrap the shrine in a sacred veil. Retro style trains run from Demachi Yanagi Station to Mt. Hiei via Yase; Kifune Shrine and Kurama are also interesting side trips.

相国寺　　　禅宗　　　　　　　　　　　　　　　　　　　　　　上京区・烏丸今出川

　鎌倉幕府の滅亡で150年ぶりに政権が京に戻った（1336年）。三代将軍・義満は室町に贅を尽くした"花の御所"で暮らし、隣接して鴨川に至る広大な地に相国寺を建立。109mの七重塔は落雷で焼失。寺は独特の声明で誦経したので"声明づら"と呼ばれた。寺には学問、書画、詩文に優れた学僧が集まり、如雪、周文、雪舟などの画僧が参禅。鶏図で知られる若沖は多数の絵画を寺に寄贈した。相国寺の東の出町は賀茂川と高野川の合流地。下鴨神社（世界遺産）が鎮座する。葵祭で行われる流鏑馬は勇壮だ。社を覆う糺の森は賀茂川の原風景を今に伝え、神さぶる空気に包まれている。出町柳駅からレトロ感覚の電車で八瀬から比叡山。貴船神社、鞍馬へ向かうのも一興だ。

Takasegawa Ichi-no-funairi

Heian-kyo needed a system for moving supplies and goods to support a population of approximately 200,000. The Kamo River flooded often and was not reliable for transport. Finally in the Edo Period, Shogun Tokugawa Ieyasu gave Ryoi Suminokura the idea to make the Kamo River more navigable by splitting off a canal. Suminokura built nine loading docks along the 11 km stretch from the capital to Fushimi and on to Osaka, and made use of small canal boats (*takasebune*). He built an estate and warehouses at Ichi-no-funairi, and the family prospered greatly by monopolizing the shipping industry. West of Kiyamachi on the banks of the Takase River are Kawaramachi-dori (Kyoto's central avenue) and the city office. Further west is Teramachi-dori, the center of town during the Meiji period. Step into some of the antique shops and eateries that have been in business for generations here. The Imperial Palace is 500 m further north.

高瀬川一之船入 運河　　　　　　　　　　　　　　中京区・西生州町

　平安京の人口は20万人ほど、大量の物資輸送が必要だった。鴨川は暴れ川で水運には向かなかった。ようやく江戸期になって角倉了以は家康に知遇を得て、鴨川の水を分流して運河を堀削した。伏見まで11km。河川で使う高瀬船を利用、荷揚げと船廻しの船入は九ヶ所に設けた。一之船入には角倉の倉庫と邸宅が一帯を占めた。都の中心地から伏見そして大阪に至る船運を独占して角倉は莫大な利益を得た。高瀬川沿いの木屋町から一筋西は京の中心街・河原町通と市役所。その西側の寺町通は明治期のメインストリートだった。老舗が多く、飲食、骨董店が続き、歩きながら店を覗くだけで楽しい。さらに500m北へ向かうと広々とした御所に至る。

Kamogawa and Noryo-yuka

Perhaps the most scenic among Kyoto's natural beauty are the purple mountains of the Higashiyama range (*Sanjuroppo*) and the clear waters of the Kamo River (*Kamogawa*). But the raging river was prone to flooding in historical times (see P63). On the outlying banks, corpses were discarded and executions even took place. Not exactly well suited for a stroll along the river. In the middle ages, though, theater and dance flourished with great popularity. Izumo no Okuni performed *kabuki* dances to a raving audience at Shijokawara. Small theaters were permitted at Yasaka Shrine, teahouses and inns soon followed, and Shijokawara became a hot spot. Cooling off by the river to escape the unbearably warm summer evenings became a longstanding custom. *Noryo-yuka*—al fresco riverside dining unique to Kyoto—evolved from such outings. How cleverly Kyoto-esque to make hot weather pleasant!

鴨川と納涼床　　　　　　　　　　　　　　　　　　　　　　　　　　　　中京区・先斗町

　山紫水明の地といえば、鴨川と東山三十六峰の風情。しかし白河法皇を悩ませた三不如意の一つ鴨川は暴れ川、度々の洪水で都人を苦しめた。古来、河原は外京なので死体を遺棄、処刑も行われた。とても川辺の散歩どころではなかった。中世以降に猿楽、蜘蛛舞などの芸能が庶民に広まった。江戸初期、出雲阿国が四条河原で演じたかぶき踊りは熱狂的な賑わいとなった。やがて八坂神社参道に芝居小屋が許可されると茶屋、旅籠が軒を連ねて遊興の地となった。うだるような京の夏、人々は河原で涼む習慣が古くからあった。その名残りがこの納涼床である。全国でもここだけ。一度はこの席で酔ってみたい。時には舞妓はんと連れ立った客もいる。この暑さも楽しみに変えるのが都人の知恵である。

先斗町　　中京区・先斗町

　江戸期に鴨川の護岸工事で出来た高瀬川との中州に旅籠(はたご)が並び、茶屋の営業が許可された。先斗町(ぽんと)は中州の先端にあり、ポルトガル語のポント(先端)に由来する。道幅わずか2m、500mほどの通りに京情緒豊かなお茶屋と赤提灯やバーが並び庶民的。時々、舞妓はんとすれ違うとさすが花街と驚く。高瀬川、木屋町へ抜ける細い路地にも店が続き、秘密めいて心が躍る。明治期に"鴨川をどり"が評判となった。その歌舞練場が三条大橋畔に建つ。四条大橋を渡ると南座。東へ歩くと祇園ならではの老舗は一見の価値あり。突き当たりは朱塗りの八坂神社。石段を上り、拝殿をさらに東へ歩くと円山公園。枝垂れ桜の巨木が枝を広げている。春ならば一度は見ておきたい桜だ。

Ponto-cho

During the 1500s, an island was formed in the Takase River from shoring up the Kamo River. Inns on the island were eventually authorized to operate for private entertainment by *maiko*. These were called ochaya (see P63). Ponto-cho, which is located at the tip of the island, probably derived its name from the Portuguese *ponto* for point. Charming *ochaya*, bars and pubs with a red paper lantern at the door can be found along the narrow street just 2 m wide and 500 m long. It is always a pleasant surprise to pass a *maiko* here. More nightspots line the alley leading to Takase River and Kiya-machi. At the Kaburenjo Theater in Sanjo Ohashi, the Kamogawa Odori dance routine performed by *maiko* has been an annual event since 1872. Cross the Shijo Ohashi Bridge to Minamiza; go east toward the traditional shops of Gion. Straight ahead is the Yasaka Shrine in red lacquer. To reach Maruyama Park where the weeping cherry in bloom is worth a visit, climb the stone steps and walk east from the altar.

Kyoto Nishiki Food Market

2015 marks the 400th anniversary of the Rinpa school of traditional Japanese art. And for the Nishiki Food Market too. In the center of Kyoto are 130 storefronts lining a 400 m stretch east to west, selling specialty foods of Kyoto and fresh seasonal delicacies. Chefs from upscale inns and restaurants source their ingredients here. The market has become a popular tourist attraction in recent years, attracting consumers and foreign tourists alike. Just browsing through the gourmet foods can be fun. Directly east of the market is Teramachi-dori. Toyotomi Hideyoshi built a line of defense in Kyogoku, the eastern edge of the city, by constructing temples in Kyoto Central within a concentrated area. A shopping arcade was built in Kyogoku to lure visitors back to a lifeless town after the capital moved to Tokyo, aiming to draw crowds to theaters, entertainment halls and restaurants. Today, students on excursion hunt for souvenirs.

錦市場

中京区・錦小路

　2015年、琳派400年の展覧会が京都国立博物館で開かれる。錦市場も400年。京都の中心部、東西400ｍほどに130の店が連なる。地下水が豊富な錦通で鮮魚の市が立ったのが最初。若狭、瀬戸内の鮮魚、干物。京野菜、丹波の乾物、湯葉に生麩、漬物と京都らしい食材が豊富だ。高級旅館、老舗料亭の板前が仕入れに来る。一般客は勿論、近年は観光地となって外国人の多いこと。高級食材を歩いて見るだけで楽しい。すぐ東が寺町通。秀吉が都の東端、京極に洛中の寺をバリケードとしてこの通りに集めた。すぐ東隣が新京極通。東京遷都で寂れた街に活気を取り戻すため、京極に歓楽街を設けた。芝居、寄席、演芸、遊技場、料理屋に人々が集まり賑わった。今は修学旅行生が歓声を上げながら土産物を探し回っている。

Nijo-jo Castle Higashi Otemon Gate

After a long history of aristocratic rule, Shogun Tokugawa Ieyasu seized bureaucratic control and built the Nijo Castle (1603) in Kyoto Central for his inaugural ceremony. The castle was also meant to strategically legitimize the Tokugawa regime (see P63). Ironically, the last shogun Yoshinobu gathered his chief vassals at Nijo Castle less than 300 years later to formally declare the restoration of Imperial rule. The citadels within the castle grounds were built in the manner of stately samurai residences; more than 3,000 magnificent works of art by painters of the Kano School adorn the interior. During the Heian Period, Shinsenen south of the castle was an imperial garden. The nearby Nijo Jinya was an inn for visiting feudal lords (*daimyo*) during the Edo Period, complete with security features such as hidden stairways and secret passageways as if it were designed for *ninjas*.

二条城・東大手門　世界遺産　　　　　　　　　　　中京区・堀川二条

　公家の長い歴史が続いた洛中に家康は五層の天守閣の二条城を築き、将軍宣下の儀式を行った。寛永期（17世紀）、後水尾天皇の二条城行幸、そして30万人を率いた家光の上洛は幕府の権威を天下に轟かせた。幕府が安定すると城は使用の必要がなく忘れ去られた。風雲急な幕末、慶喜は将軍となるも間もなく二条城に諸藩の重臣を集めて大政奉還（19世紀）を行った。城内の武家屋敷は重厚、内陣を飾る狩野派の3,000もの障屏画は豪華絢爛だ。城のすぐ南は神泉苑。平安期には皇室の庭園であった。都が大旱魃に見舞われた時、空海はここで雨乞い修法を行い見事に雨を降らせた。すぐ南には二條陣屋。大名が上洛した時の宿舎として利用された。忍者屋敷のような武者隠し、落とし階段もある。

Kitano Tenmangu Shrine

Sugawara Michizane was a scholarly minister of the Heian Court who quickly rose to prominence, only to be banished from office by a resentful aristocracy. He died of a broken spirit while in exile. When a string of disasters later fell upon Kyoto, including a fatal lightning strike on the Palace, it was superstitiously blamed on "the curse of Michizane." The Tenmangu Shrine was built in his memory to undo the curse, and the influx of school houses during the Edo Period turned Michizane into the god of education. During exam season, the shrine becomes filled with talismans (*ema*) hung by students wishing to be accepted to their school of choice. Various events have been held at the shrine throughout history: Toyotomi Hideyoshi hosted grand tea ceremonies; while Izumo no Okuni performed popular kabuki dances. In the eastern corner of the complex is a *geiko* district known as Kami-shichi-ken (see P64).

北野天満宮

上京区・馬喰町

　平安京の西北、北野は荒野で農業神の天神を祀っていた。学者の家系、菅原道真は宇多天皇の信任で右大臣に昇進。名門貴族の嫉妬から大宰府へ左遷され失意のうちに没した。その後、都に災厄が続き、清涼殿に落雷、死者まで出た。道真の祟りだと噂が広がった。道真を祀る北野天満宮を創建して世の平安を願った。境内では様々な催しが開かれ遊興の人々で賑わった。秀吉は"北野大茶湯"を催し、出雲阿国は"かぶき踊り"で爆発的な人気を得た。江戸期に寺小屋が広がると道真は学問の神様となった。受験シーズンが近づくと夥しい数の合格祈願の絵馬が奉納される。室町期に天満宮を改修した時、残った材木で七軒の茶屋を建て"上七軒"と呼ばれた。すぐ近くの西陣の旦那衆のひいきで花街は発展した。

Daitoku-ji Temple

Daito Kokushi founded Daitoku-ji in 1315 as a Zen monastery in Shibano, where noblemen used to hunt. Later, the temple flourished under the Emperors Hanazono and Go-Daigo under the disapproving eye of the Muromachi government, and structures damaged in war were rebuilt by the head priest Ikkyu Sojun. Famous tea masters such as Zuko, Sen no Rikyu, Oribe and Enshu practiced Zen at Daitoku-ji; hence "the tea temple" (*cha zura*) based on its deep association with the Way of Tea (see P64). In the 15th and 16th centuries, warlords who found solace in the tranquility of Zen and the art of the tea ceremony contributed many additions to the cloisters. Toyotomi Hideyoshi ceremoniously buried his predecessor Oda Nobunaga on the temple grounds to succeed as supreme ruler of Japan. Within the cloisters, Daisen-in houses many national treasures and important pieces of Zen art and culture. The gardens of Koto-in and Hoshun-in are exceptional. On the north side of the temple stands Imamiya Shrine, famous for the Yasurai Festival. Enjoy a panoramic view of Kyoto from Funaoka-yama at the south end, and pay a visit to the Kenkun Shrine on the east side of the mount where Nobunaga is enshrined.

大徳寺　芳春院への小径　世界遺産　禅宗　　　　　　　　　　　　　　　　北区・紫野

　紫野は公家達が狩猟に興じた地。大燈国師が紫野に結んだ小庵が大徳寺の始まり。後に花園、後醍醐天皇の帰依で発展するが室町幕府は反目した。さらに応仁の乱（1467年）で焼失。一休禅師が堺の豪商の支援で再興。そして珠光、利休、織部、遠州などの茶人が参禅して"茶づら"と呼ばれた。秀吉は信長の葬儀を大徳寺で挙行。信長の後継者をアピールして天下人となった。「動」の戦国武将は、「静」の禅文化、茶の湯に魅せられ競って塔頭を寄進した。塔頭の大仙院は方丈、絵画、枯山水などの禅文化の至宝を保持。高桐院、芳春院の庭園も素晴らしい。寺のすぐ北は今宮神社。"やすらい"は京都三奇祭の一つ。南の船岡山からは市街が一望出来る。山の東側の建勲神社には信長が祀られている。

Kinkaku-ji Temple (The Golden Pavilion)

Ashikaga Yoshimitsu left the highest office of Chancellor just three years after his appointment to retire in Kinugasa, where he built Kitayama-tei as his retirement villa and political seat. He established trade relations with the Ming Dynasty as the King of Japan, wielding power both in country and abroad. Upon his death, Kitayama-tei was converted to the Zen temple Rokuon-ji. The relic hall became The Golden Pavilion; without a doubt, its gilded magnificence is extraordinary. Down Kinukake Road west of the Pavilion, the statues of 11 of the 13 Ashikaga shoguns are on display at Toji-in Temple, the dynasty's mortuary temple built by the first Ashikaga shogun Takauji. Further west at Ryoan-ji, a study of the mysterious dry landscape garden is a must-do. A few steps more will end at the triple gates of Ninna-ji Temple.

金閣寺　世界遺産　禅宗　　　　　　　　　　　　　　　　　　　　　　　北区・衣笠

　室町幕府三代将軍・足利義満は"花の御所"を造営、相国寺を建立した。太政大臣となったが3年で辞し、衣笠に別荘の北山第を立柱。公武を超えた立場から政務の拠点とした。義満は明と国交を開き貿易を行った時、日本国王と名乗っている。義満の死後、北山第は禅寺となった。金閣寺を見た外国人はこれぞエルドラド・ジパングと映るだろう。金閣から"きぬかけの道"を西へ歩くと尊氏の菩提寺・等持院が静かに佇む。寺には2人を除く13人の歴代将軍の座像が並ぶ。尊氏、義満、義政の表情を見ると親しみがわくものだ。ここからすぐ西に龍安寺がある。ぜひとも謎に満ちた枯山水を眺め瞑想にふけるのも良い。少し西へ歩くだけで壮大な仁和寺の三門が聳える。徒然草の愉快なお坊さん達が修業した寺である。

Myoshin-ji Temple

Court nobles once kept villas with landscaped gardens and hunted in an area they called Floral Pastures (*Hanazono*) within the Myoshin-ji temple complex. The Zen priests here did not rely on the patronage of a shogun, encouraging simplicity, austerity and hard work instead. Rebuilt in 1477 after fire damage, Myoshin-ji prospered in the following years of the Muromachi Period from the sponsorship of faithful leaders of the samurai class, who enlarged the compounds and added many sub-temples. As a cost management measure for reconstruction and maintenance, the temple administrators diligently kept accounting records, and Myoshin-ji came to be known as "the abacus temple" (*soroban zura*). Noteworthy art housed within the complex include Unryuzu by Kano Tanyu in the Main Hall and the Hyonenzu ink painting by Josetsu at Taizo-in, both national treasures. The 300-year-old sal tree (*sarasoju*) at Torin-in is a beauty of nature that also symbolizes the secret to enlightenment for Zen practitioners, the concept of nothingness. Just up the path on the hill is Ninna-ji Temple.

妙心寺　世界遺産　禅宗　　　　　　　　　　　　　　　　　　　　　　　右京区・花園

　花園という雅な名は狩猟地に公家達が別荘を構え、花木を植栽して楽しんだことによる。妙心寺は五山に列せず在野を貫き質素倹約、勤行に励み"そろばんづら"と呼ばれた。寺は足利幕府の弾圧に苦しみ、応仁の乱で焼失したが、西国大名・大内氏の援助で復興。多くの武将が次々と塔頭を寄進して発展した。法堂の「雲龍図」は狩野探幽筆。退蔵院の「瓢鮎図」は不可解な禅画で知られる。東林院の樹齢300年の沙羅双樹は無常を象徴する花。寺のすぐ西は『徒然草』の吉田兼好が庵を結んだ双ケ丘。丘の遊歩道を辿ると仁和寺の堂宇がすぐ近く、眼下に望める。

Ninna-ji Temple

The cherry blossoms at Ninna-ji Temple are late bloomers. The trees do not grow much taller than three meters, either, since the root system cannot thrive in the bedrock. Under the Fujiwara clan's regency government during the Heian Period, the Emperor Uda appointed lower-ranking but brilliant Sugawara Michizane and attempted to reinstate direct imperial rule. But the Fujiwara were unyielding. The Emperor abdicated after ten years and retired as a priest in pursuit of further education and Buddhist studies while furnishing Ninna-ji with opulent art pieces. South of the elegant and formal temple, 14th century author Yoshida Kenko lived at Narabigaoka as a hermit. Amusing characters from Ninna-ji appear in his classic, *Essays in Idleness*: like the priest whose head got stuck in a pot after dancing around with it; or the abbot who was very wise but had a strange weakness for taro. Famous pottery masters in Kyoto ware (*Kyo yaki*) opened studios in front of Ninna-ji, giving the area an artsy flair.

仁和寺 世界遺産 真言宗　　　　　　　　　　　　　　　　　　　　右京区・御室

「わたしゃお多福 御室の桜 はな低くても 人が好く」。遅咲きの桜は丈が3mほど。岩盤のため根が張れない。藤原氏摂関の時代、宇多天皇は身分が低いが有能な菅原道真を登用して親政を進めるが藤原氏の壁は厚く10年で退位して出家する。御室に僧坊を営んだのが後の仁和寺。法皇は学問、仏道に励み、宸殿、書院の絢爛たる障壁画などを設え、御室御所の様相となった。寺は筆頭門蹟寺院の格式を誇る。寺のすぐ南は兼好法師が庵を結んだ双ケ丘。『徒然草』では仁和寺にありける和尚が宴会で鼎を頭に被って踊るが、鼎が抜けず大騒ぎ。大変な智者なのに桁外れの芋好きの法師など愉快な人達が登場する。門前には京焼の仁清、乾山、光琳が工房を構え、文化的な風土が育まれた。

Higashi Hongan-ji Temple

The gate in this painting—the Founder's Hall Gate (*Goei-do Mon*) of the Higashi Hongan-ji Temple—stands just north of Kyoto Station. It is one of the Three Great Gates of Kyoto. During the Kamakura Period, Shinran preached that one could enter Paradise by repeatedly reciting the Amida Buddha's name. Although popular among the masses, Shinran was persecuted by members of the more established sects, and he was forced to rove. Under Toyotomi Hideyoshi's rule, the temple was finally allowed back to Kyoto, but the faith split into East (Higashi) and West (Nishi). Tokugawa Ieyasu contributed a plot of land for the construction of the grand Higashi Hongan-ji at the current location. Directly east of the the gate along the front street are stores specializing in Buddhist artifacts. On the west stands Nishi Hongwan-ji Temple, home of Hiunkaku Pavilion, one of the three greats of Kyoto along with the Golden and Silver Pavilions. Further west, the main gate to Shimabara leads to the oldest courtesan district where elaborate banquets were held in restaurants and inns such as Sumiya, a fine example of period architecture designated as an Important Cultural Property.

東本願寺　　　真宗　　　　　　　　　　　　　　　　　　　　　　　　下京区・烏丸七条

　京都駅のすぐ北にこの壮大な御影堂門が建つ。"京都三大門"の一つ。鎌倉期に親鸞は「南無阿弥陀仏」を唱えるだけで極楽往生が出来ると説き、浄土宗は庶民から熱烈に歓迎された。旧仏教派からは激しい迫害を受け寺は各地を転々とした。秀吉の時、寺は大阪から京に戻ったが東西に分裂。家康から土地の寄進を受けて東本願寺は現在地に壮大な伽藍を営んだ。門からすぐ東の中珠数町通には仏具店が続く。その突き当たりが渉成園。広々とした池の周りは樹々が茂り茶室が静かに佇む。西本願寺（世界遺産）の飛雲閣は金閣、銀閣に並ぶ"京の三閣"。その西には島原の大門が建つ。ここは最も古い花街。置屋、揚屋が並んでいた。重文の角屋は島原の古い面影をよく残している。

東寺

世界遺産　真言宗
南区・九条町

　鉄道で京都駅に近づくと目に入るのが日本一の五重塔。平安期から旅人のランドマークだった。平安京の正面は羅城門。その東西に都を守護する官寺を建立。西寺は早くに焼失した。9世紀、嵯峨天皇から下賜された東寺を空海は真言密教の根本道場とした。密教は言葉で説明し難い。密教世界を絵にしたのが曼荼羅図。空海は二十一尊の仏像を講堂に安置して立体曼荼羅を実現。この曼荼羅界は圧巻である。毎月21日は"弘法さん"と呼ばれる市に1,000もの露店が境内狭しと並び市民が訪れる。食品、衣料、花木そして骨董品も楽しみだ。東寺の4km東に朱塗りの伏見稲荷大社が鎮座する。遷都以前の古社。大社は官寺である東寺の鎮守の社という関係にある。春には東寺と周辺で稲荷大社の祭礼が行なわれる。

To-ji Temple

 As the train approaches Kyoto Station, the To-ji Pagoda comes into view. This landmark for travelers since the Heian Period is the tallest wooden structure in Japan today. To-ji (East Temple) and Sai-ji (West Temple) were built to protect the ancient capital, flanking Rashomon Gate at the center of Heian-kyo. Sai-ji did not to survive long, but Master Priest Kukai (Kobo Daishi) established To-ji as the main school for esoteric Buddhism in the ninth century. The highlight of the temple is located in the main hall. A three-dimensional mandala of 21 Buddha statues were designed by Kukai to help visualize the philosophical concept of esoteric Buddhism that was otherwise difficult to explain. The temple holds a flea market called Kobo-san on the 21st of each month, showcasing more than 1,000 vendors selling food, clothing, plants and antiques. To-ji is surrounded by the sacred grove of Fushimi Inari-taisha, an ancient Shinto shrine predating Kyoto and known for the visual explosion of red lacquer. A thanksgiving ceremony held by the shrine in the spring takes place on the entire grounds covering both To-ji and Inari Shrine.

洛東 Kyoto East

Tofuku-ji Temple

Crossing a sea of maples through a covered bridge (*Gaun-kyo*) to enter the grounds of Tofuku-ji Temple pleasantly surprises every visitor, especially in the fall when the leaves show off their spectacular foliage. During the Heian Period, the politically dominant Northern branch of the Fujiwara clan that had exclusively held the most powerful positions in government split into several families. Among them, the Kujo Family sought to show their supremacy and built Tofuku-ji, naming it after the two great To-ji and Kofuku-ji temples. The buildings and halls are indeed the grandest in Kyoto, and locals in-the-know have affectionately referred to Tofuku-ji as "The Monastery" (*garan zura*). Crossing another covered bridge (*Tsuten-kyo*) to reach the Founder's Hall (*Kaisando*) from the main hall, it feels like a walk in the clouds surrounded by thousands of the hallmark maple trees; not a single cherry blossom tree here (see P64).

東福寺・通天橋　　　禅宗　　　　　　　　　　　　　　　　　　　　　　東山区・月輪

　東福寺入口の日下門へ向かうと屋根付の臥雲橋を渡る。ふと開けた方を見ると楓の海を渡る橋に驚かされる。摂政、関白を独占してきた藤原北家は荘園の相続で近衛家と九条家に分裂。九条家が優位を誇示せんと東福寺を建立。東大寺と興福寺を併せた壮大な名。伽藍は京都最大の偉容を誇る。京雀は"伽藍づら"と呼ぶ。谷を越え開山堂へ向かう通天橋を渡ると天空を歩むような錯覚を覚える。2,000本の楓が寺の象徴。桜は一本も無い。寺のすぐ東の泉涌寺は"御寺"と尊称される別格の寺。十三代にわたる天皇陵と陵墓が並ぶ皇室の菩提寺。戦後まで700年間も門を閉ざしてきた。寺の大門から坂を下る、山に囲まれた擂鉢の底状の平地に建つ壮大な伽藍配置には意表を衝かれる。

Kiyomizu-dera Temple

Standing on the expansive deck off the main hall of Kiyomizu Temple to view the entire city in one sweep, the piercing voices from visiting school groups echo in the ravine below. The Emperor Kanmu forbade the construction or moving of unofficial temples when Kyoto became the capital, but an exception was made for Kiyomizu Temple when one of his generals (Sakanoue no Tamuramaro) and a Nanto Buddhist priest from Nara placed a statue of the *Kannon Bosatsu* in the Otowa no Taki waterfall. Commoners worshipped the *Kannon Bosatsu* as a savior from daily hardship. Other dieties were added in time, and worshippers of all faiths would gather. The spacious grounds have long provided an ideal respite while admiring the cherry blossoms or autumn foliage over a cup of tea. The slopes around Kiyomizu were well-suited for climbing kilns, and the area became a large production site for Kiyomizu ware (*Kiyomizu-yaki*), attracting a number of legendary potters and ceramic artists. Browse the china shops along Teapot Lane (*Chawan zaka*) and spend some time at Kawai Kanjiro Memorial Museum to see an actual climbing kiln.

清水寺　世界遺産　北法相宗　　　　　　　　　　　　　　　　　　　　　山科区・清水

　清水の舞台に立つと市街が一望出来て晴れ晴れする。修学旅行生の甲高い声が谷に響き渡る。桓武天皇は平安京遷都では官寺以外は寺の建設、移設も禁じた。南都の僧と坂上田村麻呂将軍が音羽の滝に観音像を安置して既に建造中だった清水寺は例外となった。庶民の苦悩を救済して下さる慈悲深い観音信仰が広がり病気平癒、縁結びに安産、多様な仏像が祀られ貴賤を問わず人々は寺に詣で祈った。広い境内で桜、紅葉を賞で、茶店で休み遊興の地ともなった。清水の斜面を利用して登り窯が築かれ、古くから清水焼の一大産地となった。頴川、清水六兵衛、青木木米など多くの名工が活躍した。茶碗坂には優美な陶芸店が並ぶ。五条坂の南西500ｍには"登り窯"が残る河井寬次郎記念館は趣がある。

三年坂

伝統的建造物群保存地区

東山区・清水

　清水は坂の町。清水坂と五条坂の交差点で北へ下る急な石段が三年坂。急坂に古い民家がひしめき合う。少し歩くと緩い坂の二年坂。この辺りは江戸から大正頃までの虫籠窓、数寄屋造りの古い建物が続く。甘味処、食事処、土産物、伝統工芸品店と京情緒たっぷりのおもてなしだ。大正期の抒情画家・竹久夢二は画学生の彦乃とこの地で暮らしたが、彦野は結核により25歳の若さで月夜の宵待草のように儚く散った。高台寺の高台に沿って東へ向かうと維新の道。坂本龍馬、中岡慎太郎、木戸孝允はじめ維新の志士達の墓が並ぶ。若い人達の墓参が多いのには驚く。

Sannenzaka

Kiyomizu is a town of hills. At the intersection of Kiyomizu-zaka and Gojo-zaka, steep stone steps head north. This is Sannenzaka, where older homes are crowded into the hill. A few steps ahead is the more gentle slope of Ninenzaka. Here the houses have traditional architectural details such as open rooms and louvered windows typical of the Edo to Taisho Periods. Shops offer sweets, traditional dishes, souvenirs, arts and crafts. Takehisa Yumeji (the famous romance poet and painter from the Taisho Period) lived in Kiyomizu with art student and muse Hikono, who perished like a fleeting evening primrose in moonlight when she was just 25 years young. Walking east along Kodai-ji Temple will lead to Ishin-no-michi, where the graves of heroes who fought to restore imperial rule—Sakamoto Ryoma, Nakaoka Shintaro, Kido Koin—are visited by a surprising number of young visitors.

Yasaka Pagoda

Climbing uphill on Yasaka Street from Higashi-oji, the Yasaka Pagoda begins to loom high above. Officially Hokan-ji Temple, the pagoda is its main structure built in the 6th century by Prince Shotoku. It is the oldest temple in Kyoto, burned down and rebuilt many times. What had eventually fallen into a state of disrepair was revitalized when government-approved bordellos opened in the area during the Edo Period. Down the hill west of Yasaka Street is Kennin-ji Temple, famous for Tawaraya Sotatsu's greatest art work, *The Wind and Thunder Gods*. About 300 m south of this dignified temple is Rokuharamitsu-ji Temple, which houses the statue of priest Kuya Shonin with six tiny Buddha figures projecting from his mouth At one time, the Taira clan established Rokuhara as their palace compound with as many as 3,000 residences. When the rival Minamoto stormed upon Kyoto toward the end of the Heian Period, the Taira clan set their homes on fire before fleeing to western Japan.

八坂の塔　　　　禅宗　　　　　　　　　　　　　　　　　　　　　　　　　東山区・清水

　東大路から八坂通の坂を上ると八坂の塔は迫ってくるような高さ。塔だけの寺である。飛鳥期（7世紀）に聖徳太子の創建と伝える寺。京都で最も古い寺だ。清水寺と八坂神社の境界争いで何度も焼失、再建を繰り返し応仁の乱で周辺は荒廃した。江戸期に遊女屋が認められてようやく活気を取り戻した。八坂通を西へ坂を下ると建仁寺。宗達筆の「風神雷神図」で知られる寺の伽藍は壮大だ。寺から300m南に歩けば六波羅蜜寺。口から小さな六体の仏様を吐くユニークな空也上人像で著名な寺である。この六波羅に住み着き、勢力を拡大したのが平氏一族。館は3,000を超えたとも。源氏が上洛すると六波羅第と呼ばれた館群は平氏が自ら火を放って西国へ落ちて行った。

Nene-no-Michi

A short 500 m stretch from Yasaka Shrine just north of Kiyomizu Temple is Nene no Michi, a main tourist aisle leading to Kodai-ji Temple by climbing eastward and uphill on Daidokoro-zaka from Entoku-ji Temple. Kodai-ji is a Zen temple established for her parents by Nene, Toyotomi Hideyoshi's widow also known as Kita no Mandokoro. Nene spent her later years at Kodai-ji as a priestess deep in mourning. The temple is well known for its cherry blossoms, autumn foliage and seasonal sweets called *hagi*. Teahouses built in architectural styles favored by Hideyoshi were moved to the property from other locations. The gilded lacquer (*Kodai-ji Makie*) adorning some of the buildings' interior is magnificent. Hideyoshi's retainers who adored Nene visited her often here. When Hideyoshi lost his final battle in the summer of 1615, Nene could have sighted the smoke from Osaka Castle southwest. From Nene no Michi, a narrow winding stone path continues where upscale restaurants and inns specializing in private dining have for years catered to a clientele in econo-political circles holding discreet dinner meetings. Perhaps the locals might whisper, "*dango-koji*" (price-fixing street) when they mention this location…

ねゝの道

東山区・下河原町

　八坂神社から南の清水寺へ向かう500ｍほどの"ねゝの道"は観光のメインルート。円徳院から東の急な台所坂を上ると高台寺。北の政所ねゝが親の菩提を弔うために建立、そして秀吉を偲んで過ごした禅寺である。寺は桜、紅葉、萩の名所。桃山城から移した傘亭、時雨亭は秀吉好みの茶室。高台寺蒔絵は豪華絢爛だ。足軽時代からの秀吉の大勢の家臣がねゝを訪れた。しかし大阪夏の陣（1615年）で秀頼と淀殿は自害。ねゝは寺からはるか西南の彼方に落城の煙を見ていたかもしれない。ねゝの道から細い石畳の曲がりくねった路地が続く石塀小路は、数寄屋造りの料亭、旅館などが続き静寂そのもの。京雀は談合小路と囁く。

Kyoto Minamiza Theatre

Billboards go up for the new season at Minamiza Theatre in December. Centuries earlier, crowds went wild at Shijokawara back when Izumo no Okuni performed kabuki dances (1603). Inns and teahouses sprang up along the path leading to Kitano Tenmangu Shrine as the predecessor to Gion. On Shijo Street, the Ichiriki Teahouse is a landmark associated with the legendary *47 Ronin*. Hanami-oji has many teahouses, haute cuisine restaurants (*ryotei*) and some very old shops. It is the most celebrated *geiko* sector where you might meet a *maiko* (see P64). Kenjin-ji Temple to the south is known as "the academic temple" (*gakumon zura*). Straight through the spacious grounds about 200 m west leads to the Miyagawa-cho neighborhood. This is another *geiko* district, a bit more quiet and subtle.

南座・顔見世興行

東山区・川端四条

　南座に顔見世の招きが上がると京の師走が始まる。出雲阿国が北野天満宮での"かぶき踊り"に次いで四条河原で舞台を設けると熱狂的な賑わいとなった（1603年）。その姿は奇抜、異相、異風の傾奇者。やがて八坂神社の参道に七軒の小屋が建つと茶屋、旅籠が軒を連ねて祇園町が形成されてゆく。南座は江戸からの伝統を守り通した唯一の劇場。東の八坂神社へ向かうと祇園町北と南を結ぶ花見小路の角の豪壮な"一力亭"は忠臣蔵でお馴染みの茶屋だ。花見小路はお茶屋、料亭、老舗が並び、時には舞妓はんとすれ違う華やかな花街だ。すぐ南は壮大な伽藍が聳える建仁寺。京雀は"学問づら"と呼んだ。寺の広い境内を突き抜け、200ｍも西へ歩けば宮川町の花街。渋味のある静かな町並みである。

Gion Shinbashi

The teahouses on Shinbashi-dori belong to a preservation district that is protected under Japan's cultural heritage laws. When the cherry blossoms are in season, the street is full of tourists busy with their cameras. West of the quaint little Tatsumi Shrine in a spot where the teahouse Daitomo used to be, there is a rock carved with the first line of a poem by Yoshii Isamu. The mistress of the teahouse was known as quite the literature fan. Yoshii loved to travel and he liked to drink, spending many a night at Daitomo with other writers who also chose Kyoto as the setting for their literary masterpieces. Gion at night is something special. It is an exclusive circle, hard to get in. But a small pub tucked away in the tightly knit row of houses at the end of a maze of alleys can just as well impart a sense of luxury. Pub food is great. Drinks are fine. And there is ambience. Gion, cherished and nurtured by exclusivity, abounds with the elegance and vogue of Kyoto.

祇園新橋の桜 　　　　　　　　　　　　　　　　　　　　　　　　　　　東山区・祇園

　お茶屋が並ぶ新橋通は伝統的建造物群保存地区。祇園を流れる白川沿いの桜が咲くと観光客が押し寄せ、皆さんシャッターを押すのに忙しい。小さな巽神社のすぐ西、お茶屋・大友の跡地に吉井勇の歌碑が建つ。大友の女将は文学好きで知られる。吉井は酒と旅を愛した紅燈歌人。大友によく泊まり、多くの作家も訪れた。与謝野晶子も祇園の歌を多く残している。祇園は華やぐ夜が良い。しかし格の高い所だから気楽にとはいかない。家が建て込み迷路のような路地の奥にある秘密めいた安い居酒屋も楽しい。年に１、２度友人達と祇園で呑む。店の設えが違う。料理も酒も上等。贅沢な気分になれる。京の旦那衆が育んできた町。京の雅、粋が集約されている。

Chion-in Temple

Just north of the weeping cherries at Maruyama Park, the sanmon at Chion-in Temple presents itself as the greatest gate structure in Japan. Upon entering, stone steps point the way up to the magnificent Mieido Hall. Chion-in started out as Master Priest Honen's meditation hut nearby, where he preached salvation. He was 43 before he left training on Mt. Hiei. Honen's teachings were extremely popular among the masses despite persecution by the more established sects. Tokugawa Ieyasu expanded the temple grounds in order to place his mother to rest. The Seven Wonders of Chion-in would be fun to explore. On New Year's Eve, a team of 17 monks ring the temple bell. Next to Chion-in, the camphor trees are 800 years old at the Shoren-in Temple. Some examples of what make this imperial temple serene: gardens designed by master landscapers, the Kogosho living quarters, a pond designed in the shape of a dragon (*Ryujin no Ike*). The Painting of the Blue Cetaka (*Ao Fudo Myo-o*) is a national treasure; one of the three Wisdom Kings (*Sanfudo*) along with the red and yellow cetakas.

知恩院　　浄土宗　　　　　　　　　　　　　　　　　　　　　　　　　　　東山区・林下町

　円山公園の枝垂れ桜のすぐ北に日本最大という知恩院の三門が聳える。山門を通り険しい石段を上るとこれまた壮大な御影堂。17人もの僧が打ち鳴らす除夜の梵鐘の轟音はちっぽけな煩悩を粉砕してくれる。知恩院七不思議を探しながら境内を訪ねるのも楽しみだ。専修念仏を説いた法然が43歳で叡山を下り、東山吉水で庵を結んだのが知恩院の始まり。多くの庶民に支持されたが旧仏教派からは迫害を受けることとなる。家康は母の菩提を弔うため、広大な寺領を寄進して寺は発展した。北隣は門蹟寺院・青蓮院。入口の大楠は樹齢800年。竜の如く太い枝葉が空を覆う。相阿弥、小堀遠州の庭園、御所から移された典雅な建物を坐して眺めると静けさが体に染み入る。寺宝の青不動は黄、赤に並ぶ三不動の一つだ。

Nanzen-ji Temple

East of the Heian Shrine and Okazaki's cultural facilities, the main entrance (*sanmon*) at Nanzen-ji Temple is one of the Three Great Gates of Kyoto. This one, in particular, is famous for outlaw Ishikawa Goemon's hiding place and for a scene from the kabuki play about him. Once there were more than 1,000 resident monks before the temple was destroyed in the Onin War. It was restored during the Edo Period by abbot Ishin Suden, who was commended for his efforts and promoted to a Tokugawa advisor. His battle plan for the Siege of Osaka (1615) defeated the Toyotomi clan. Nanzen-ji is called "the samurai temple" (*buke zura*). The dry landscape gardens are fabulous, as is the collection of more than 3,000 silk and gold leaf screens painted by artists of the Kano School. Autumn colors are gorgeous at the Eikando Temple nearby. Go eastward up the hill to reach the Philosopher's Path. The Silver Pavilion (Ginkaku-ji) will be close (see P64).

南禅寺　　　禅宗　　　　　　　　　　　　　　　　　　　　　　　　　　　右京区・南禅寺

　平安神宮、京都市美術館、図書館、ロームシアター、みやこめっせ、動物園という文化ゾーンの岡崎からすぐ東が南禅寺。京都三大門の三門は歌舞伎で石川五右衛門が「絶景かな」と見得を切る場面で周知である。1,000人もの僧が起居した寺だが応仁の乱で焼失した。江戸期、以心崇伝が寺を再興。家康にその手腕を買われ、黒衣の宰相として活躍。大阪夏の陣を画策して豊臣を滅亡させた。京雀は"武家づら"と呼ぶ。寺の方丈、天授庵の枯山水は見事だ。狩野派の障屏画は3,000点にものぼる。ローマの水道橋を模した琵琶湖疎水の水路閣は異質だが今や境内の名所。寺には名水が湧く。江戸期から湯豆腐は名物だった。北隣は永観堂。紅葉のシーズンは大変な人出となる。寺から坂を東へ上ると哲学の道。銀閣寺も近い。

Honen-in Temple

Heading east from the Philosopher's Path (*Tetsugaku no Michi*) and uphill to Honen-in Temple, the simply constructed gate (*sanmon*) with a thatched roof is totally unexpected. Here, Honen and his disciples built a small hut for prayer (*nenbutsu*), isolated from the castigating eyes of conventional Buddhism. Once inside, mounds of white sand with designs (*byakusadan*) symbolize water on either side of the path. They evoke a sense of purification as time passes quietly under the maple leaves glistening in the sun. South at Anraku-ji Temple, named for one of Honen's disciples, the *sanmon* also has a thatched roof and the grounds are just as understated. The Cloister Emperor Gotoba executed Anraku and Oren as repercussion for losing two of his favorite consorts to the faith. Honen and Shinran were also exiled as punishment. The hill to the east of Honen-in is Yoshidayama. The Yoshida Shrine is famous for a festival in February (*setsubun*). At Kyoto University, the campus cafe serves a tasty dish named Socho Curry.

法然院　　　浄土宗　　　　　　　　　　　　　　　　　　　　　　　　　　左京区・鹿ヶ谷

　観光客が行き交う哲学の道から東へ坂を上ると法然院。法然が弟子と共に迫害を避け、人里離れた地で念仏修業を行った草庵が始まり。森の中の参道を行くと茅葺の山門は素朴で意外に感じる。門の石段下の紋様が描かれた一対の白砂壇(びゃくしゃだん)は"水"を表し、歩くだけで心身が清められる趣向だ。降り注ぐ光に映える楓、静かに静かに時が流れている。すぐ南の安楽寺も茅葺の山門。後鳥羽上皇寵愛の二人の女官が専修念仏に惹かれ出家する。上皇は弟子の安楽と住蓮を死罪、高齢の法然、親鸞を流罪とした。東に見える岡は吉田山（神楽岡）。東麓に吉田神社が鎮座する。節分の日は大勢の参拝者で賑わう。その隣に広がるのが京都大学のキャンパス。レストランの総長カレーが評判だ。

Ginkaku-ji Temple (The Silver Pavilion)

Ashikaga Yoshimasa, the eighth shogun of the Muromachi Period, endured meddlesome in-laws over succession rights. After he named his younger brother Yoshimi as successor, wife Tomiko gave birth to their son Yoshihisa. Naturally, she wanted their son to be the heir. A dispute over the succession led to the Onin War (1467-77), burning Kyoto to the ground. It was a pointless war that remained at an impasse. Meanwhile, Yoshimasa built the future Silver Pavilion (*Higashiyama-den*) as his villa and spent his time in leisurely pursuits, just as Mad King Ludwig II exhausted his personal fortune building castles in Bavaria. Directly south of Ginkaku-ji is Honen-in Temple. A short way down the hill, the Philosopher's Path (named after philosopher Nishida Ikutaro of Kyoto University) runs along Lake Biwa Canal. Seasonal flora, greenery and the sound of trickling water create a refreshing atmosphere.

銀閣寺　世界遺産　禅宗　　　　　　　　　　　　　　　　　左京区・浄土寺

　細川、山名などの大大名、妻の富子の実家・日野家等々の幕政干渉に苦しんだ八代将軍・義政は弟の義視を後継者として隠棲。その直後に富子は義尚を出産。富子は我が子を将軍にしようと義視と対立。後継争いは守護大名を巻き込み東西に分裂。応仁の乱（1467年）となり都は焦土と化した。勝者も敗者もない全く不毛の戦乱だった。義政は東山殿を建て、学問、諸芸、作庭の日々。国政を傾けて城造りに明け暮れたバイエルン王・ルートヴィヒⅡ世と同じだ。銀閣寺のすぐ南は法然院。茅葺の山門と紋様が描かれた白砂壇は印象深い。ここから少し坂を下ると琵琶湖疎水に沿った"哲学の道"。京都帝大の哲学者・西田幾太郎が好んで散歩した小径。季節の花々、緑に包まれた道と流れは爽やかな空気に包まれている。

Artistic Signage
姉小路の老舗
中京区・姉小路

Antique signage on old storefronts along Anekoji Street feature actual art strokes done by famous artists like Kitaoji Rosanjin and Tomioka Tessai.
老舗の看板には魯山人や鉄斎の書が使われている。

Around town
京の町角

Local Produce
京野菜

Locally grown vegetables turn into delicious Kyoto specialties such as *senmaizuke* pickled turnips made from *Shogoin kabura*, grilled eggplants with miso glaze made from *Kamo nasu*, and stewed squash made from *Shishigatani kabocha*.
聖護院かぶらは千枚漬、賀茂なすは田楽、鹿ヶ谷かぼちゃは煮付けにすると美味。

Clarke Memorial Hall, Doshisha University
同志社大学・クラーク記念館　上京区・烏丸今出川

Summer maidens
夏の乙女

Kyoto fashionistas might spend every last yen for the pleasure of dressing up in their finest kimonos (*Kyo no kidaore*).
京の着だおれ。

洛北 Kyoto North

Mt. Hiei

Mt. Hiei (848 m) lies northeast of Kyoto, in the direction of the demons' gate (*kimon*). Saicho established the Tendai monastery Enryaku-ji on the mountain to protect Heian-kyo (see P64). The East Pagoda (*To-do*), the West Pagoda (*Sai-to*) and Yokawa are accessible by shuttle bus. At the western foot of the mountain is the imperial villa, Shugakuin Rikyu. At the eastern foot of the mountain in the temple town of Sakamoto, beautiful masonry walls surround monks' residences (*satobo*). The local mason's guild (*Ano-shu*) laid the stones to Osaka Castle. Hiyoshi Taisha, the guardian shrine for Enryaku-ji, is set deep within the forest. Mt. Hiei goes through many seasonal changes. Once the yellowed leaves fall, snow starts to flurry. And when cold winds blow down from the mountain, Kyoto shivers from *hiei oroshi*.

植物園から望む比叡山 滋賀県・大津市

　比叡山（848ｍ）は平安京の鬼門にあたる。この山を都の鎮守とし、最澄は天台宗・延暦寺を開いた。寺は公貴族の庇護で発展する。荒法師が強大となり、白河天皇の三不如意の一つとなった。僧侶には全山が修業の場、"千日回峰"という荒業で知られる。山で修業した法然、栄西、親鸞、道元、日蓮は一宗一派の開祖となった。東塔、西塔、横川と広大な地域に塔頭が広がり、巡回バスが利用出来る。山の西麓には修学院離宮が広がる。東麓は門前町の坂本。寺僧が住む"里坊（さとぼう）"は美しい石垣が続く。すぐ近くの穴太衆（あのう）が大阪城の石垣を築いている。延暦寺の鎮守社、日吉大社は深い森の中に鎮座する。叡山は季節ごとに様々に変容する。黄葉が散ると雪が散りつき、比叡おろしが吹き荒れると京雀は震え上がる。

社家町　　北区・上賀茂

上賀茂神社は五穀豊穣、地上の穢れを祓う荒ぶる賀茂別雷神を祀る。勅祭である葵祭が催行される上賀茂神社、下鴨神社（世界遺産）は桓武天皇により王城鎮護の社とされた。社家は賀茂氏ゆかりの神官の住居である。聖なる明神川の水を邸内に引き入れ、禊水、池水に用いて再び川に戻す。社殿を見下すことを遠慮して土塀、平屋の質素な佇まいだ。すぐ近くの太田神社の杜若群落（天然記念物）は葵祭の頃、一面を紫色に染める。さらに1.5kmほど東の圓通寺には比叡山を借景とする枯山水がある。徳川幕府に翻弄された後水尾上皇は庭を眺め憂を癒していた。王朝文化の香り高い寺である。寺から1km南の深泥池は1万年も前から堆積した水生植物群の宝庫（天然記念物）である。

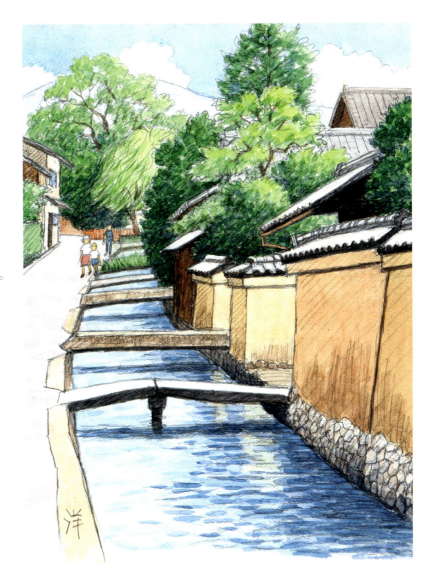

Shake-machi

Kamigamo Shrine—known for the Hollyhock Festival (*Aoi Matsuri*)—is devoted to the thunder god (*Wakeikazuchi*) who protects the five grains of nature's bounty (*Gokoku Hojo*). The Emperor Kanmu designated Kamigamo and Shimogamo Shrines as Imperial Shrines. The Kamo clansmen (one of the sacerdotal families of Japan) are the shrine keepers, and their residence is known as *shake*. Rather than perching itself high, the residence is a humble single story with walls made of wattle and daub from natural clay. A stream from the sacred Myojin River runs through the compound. The water is used for ritual purification and collected in a pond before returning to the river. At the nearby Ota Shrine, fields of purple Japanese irises bloom around the time of Aoi Matsuri. About 1.5 km further east, a dry landscape garden takes advantage of Mt. Hiei as the backdrop at Entsu-ji Temple. The Emperor Go-Mizuno-o would gaze at the garden to seek comfort from the oppressive Tokugawa government. The temple itself exemplifies the culture of Heian Court. The floating bog of Mizoroga Pond (*Mizoroga-ike*) 1 km south of Entsu-ji is a treasure trove of aquatic plant deposits from 10,000 years ago.

Sanzen-in Temple

Seafood from northern Fukui was delivered to Kyoto on the Mackerel Road (*Saba Kaido*). Along the way was Ohara, a small basin at the northern foot of Mt. Hiei. Coming or going, the trip went through the mountains. Sanzen-in Temple was at first a Tendai training temple for chanting the sutra. Many women visited for worship since it was the only temple open to them. The Hall was built by the 29-year-old grief-stricken widow of a Fujiwara clansman, who threw herself into work and ardent prayer. It is a simple building with a clapboard roof. The statue of the Amida Trinity (*Amida Sanzon*) has a compassionate expression. At Hosen-in Temple nearby, the Bankan-en garden features a different frame of view depending on where the viewer sits. The blood-stained ceiling was repurposed from the dismantled Fushimi Castle after the siege. Raigo-in, Shorin-in, Jikko-in are also temples worth visiting. Kochidani is a small mountain village about 2 km north. The Amida-ji Temple at this village, with a gate fashioned after the Ryugu Castle, is a famous spot for autumn foliage. Beyond, Yamanaka-goe leads north to the tiny beach of Wakasa Bay, and to the East down the hill is the Lake Biwa Ohashi.

大原三千院・往生極楽院　　　　　天台宗　　　　　　　　　　　　　　左京区・大原来迎院町

　京に若狭の海産物を運んだ道が鯖街道。その道筋、比叡山の北麓の小さな盆地が大原。行くも戻るも山の中。三千院は天台宗の声明道場が始まり。寺は唯一、女性に開かれたので多くの女性が訪れ祈った。柿葺の質素な往生極楽院は29歳の真如房尼が建立、ひたすら亡夫のために念仏、勤行に励んだ。三体の阿弥陀三尊像はおおらかな表情だ。宝泉院の額縁庭園は坐る位置を変えるだけで風景が変わる。上を見上げると伏見城が襲われた時の血天井に驚かされる。来迎院、勝林院、実光院の塔頭も巡りたい。寺から北へ2kmが古知谷。素朴な山間の集落である。竜宮城のような門の阿弥陀寺は紅葉の名所として知られる。この先は山中越、さらに北へ進めば若狭湾の小浜。山中越から東へ坂を下ると琵琶湖大橋である。

Ohara in Autumn

Kyoto has long been supplied with charcoal from the countryside of Ohara, where narrow paths are framed by hedges, shrubs and stone walls covered in moss. Bengala, a natural red dye, colors the wooden frames of the houses. A few thatched roofs remain here and there. Very rustic. The mountainside, a bubbling brook, seasonal flora, abundant nature—these are the charms of Ohara. In the summer, fields of lotus blossoms and dandelions are dotted with the fiery red specks of Japanese basil (*shiso*). Pickled vegetables seasoned with *shiso*, called *shibazuke*, became a local specialty after an attendant to Kenreimon-in Tokuko found a way to preserve the summer crop (more on Tokuko at P40, Jakko-in Temple). Local women called *Ohara-me*, dressed in indigo-dyed cotton or wool kimonos sashed with red obi, used to walk to the ancient capital to sell fresh vegetables and *shibazuke*. The traditional dress of *Ohara-me* is said to be modeled after the field clothes worn by Awanonaiji, Tokuko's attendant.

大原の秋

左京区・大原

　大原は古くから炭焼きの里、薪炭を都に運んでいた。大原の細い道には苔むした石垣、生垣と庭木。家屋の木組はベンガラ色。少なくなったが茅葺の家も残り、鄙びた佇まいだ。山並みと高野川のせせらぎ、季節の花々、豊かな自然が大原の魅力。れんげやたんぽぽが咲いていた田畑は夏になると赤く燃えるような紫蘇の畑があちらこちらで見られる。平家の落人・建礼門院徳子は寂光院で静かに平家一門の菩提を弔う日々。彼女に仕えた阿波内侍が夏野菜を紫蘇に漬け込んだのが"しば漬け"。藍染めの絣に赤い帯の大原女が柴、野菜などを頭上に載せ、都で売り歩いた。そして得意先に配った"しば漬け"が徐々に評判となり大原名物となった。大原女姿は阿波内侍の野良着を村人が真似たものという。

雪の寂光院　　天台宗
左京区・大原草生

　自然豊かな大原は隠れ里でもある。清盛の娘・徳子は高倉天皇の中宮となる。生まれた子は3歳で安徳天皇。清盛は外戚という絶頂期を迎える。しかし後白河法皇の画策で木曽義仲が都に迫ると平氏は自ら居館に火を放って西国へと落ちた。義経は壇ノ浦まで平氏を追い、建礼門院徳子は8歳の安徳天皇、母と共に入水するが源氏の兵に引き上げられ、京に戻された。徳子は剃髪して寂光院の粗末な庵で我が子と平氏一門の冥福を祈る日々。戦で死んでゆく平氏と源氏の武将達が語られる『平家物語』。最終章は安徳天皇の祖父・後白河法皇が徳子を訪ねる"大原御幸"。あまりにも哀れな徳子の姿、「六道のすべてを見ました」と徳子は語り法皇は涙した。

Jakko-in Temple

Nature has always flourished in Ohara. It was also once a refuge. Kenreimon-in Tokuko was the daughter of Taira Kiyomori and wife of Emperor Takakura. Her son ascended to the throne as Emperor Antoku at the age of three, and Kiyomori's power reached its peak as the Emperor's maternal grandfather. But the Emperor Antoku's paternal grandfather, the Cloistered Emperor Go-Shirakawa, schemed against Kiyomori and persuaded the rival Minamoto clan to raid the capital. The Taira set their own compound ablaze and fled to the western provinces. Minamoto Yoshitsune pursued the Taira army to Dan no Ura. Tokuko, her mother and the 8-year-old Emperor Antoku plunged to their deaths, but Tokuko was pulled out of the ocean by a Minamoto warrior and she was forcibly returned to Kyoto. Tokuko shaved her head, became a nun and led a meager existence in reclusive prayer at Jakko-in, mourning for her lost son and family members. In the last chapter of *The Tales of the Heike*, a martial epic of the Taira and Minamoto warriors, the Cloistered Emperor Go-Shirakawa visits Tokuko at Ohara only to find her in such a destitute state that it brings tears to his eyes.

Kitayama Cedars

Shuzan Kaido winds through Kitayama, Tanba and on to Wakasa Bay. The cedar (*sugi*) grown in this area has been in great demand for *sukiya* architecture, thanks to the popularity of the Way of Tea. Temperate waters of the Kiyotaki River and the natural shield from harsh winds are ideal for forest lumber. During the careful growth process, the lower branches are pruned so the beautiful long legs of cedar trunks can continue growing on the steep slopes. Once the trees are felled and the bark is stripped, the logs are polished with river sand and left to air dry in cold winds. This develops the distinct luster. Further north on the mountain road past Shuzan, the quaint village of Miyama with thatched roof houses by the Yura River have the same roof lines as those in Tanba. The cluster of storybook houses are actually terraced on the hillside; imagine *Tales of Old Japan*. In the town of Takao by the Kiyotaki River, well-known Jingo-ji, Saimyo-ji and Kosan-ji Temples have attracted autumn foliage viewers since the Heian Period. Regrettably the roads get very congested today.

北山杉の郷 周山街道

北区・京北町中川

　周山街道は北山、丹波山地を縫って若狭湾に至る。北山杉は茶の湯の流行で数寄屋造りに重宝されてきた銘木。中川を中心とする北山は清滝川の湿度と強風がなく適地である。急斜面の植林は下枝を払って丁寧に育てる。整然と並ぶ杉の幹は脚線美のよう。伐採後は皮を剥ぎ、川砂で丹念に磨き上げ、寒風に晒すと独特の光沢が出る。街道をさらに北へ向かうと周山。由良川に沿って東へ行くと"茅葺の里"・美山である。丹波型の同じ造りの茅葺屋根が雛壇状に並んで"日本昔ばなし"の世界となっている。清滝川沿いの高雄は神護寺、西明寺、高山寺の名刹が続き、平安期から紅葉狩りを楽しんだ名所。秋は車の渋滞で大変だ。

The Hojo Garden at Ryoan-ji
龍安寺方丈庭園
右京区・龍安寺

The dry landscape garden was designed for meditation and zazen.
枯山水の庭は、瞑想、座禅の場として造形された。

Tenjuan Garden at Nanzen-ji
天授庵庭園
左京区・南禅寺

At the temples
京の庭園・仏像

Statue of the Amida Nyorai
阿弥陀如来坐像
宇治市・宇治

The image of the *Amida Nyorai* at Byodo-in Temple was created by master sculptor Jocho Busshi in the 10th century. Jocho's style and technique shaped Japanese religious statuary art during the 10th and 11th centuries.
平等院。定朝作

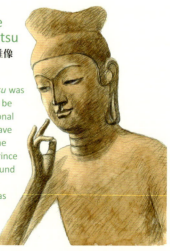

Statue of the Miroku Bosatsu
弥勒菩薩半跏思惟像
右京区・太秦

The *Miroku Bosatsu* was the first artifact to be designated a National Treasure. It may have been a gift from the Korean Court to Prince Shotoku Taishi around the 7th century. Koryu-ji Temple was built to enshrine the image.
広隆寺

Aoi Festival
葵祭　上京区・京都御所

The imperial envoy leads a procession of 500 people from the Imperial Palace to the Shimogamo and Kamigamo Shrines.

5月15日、勅使以下500名が御所を出発して下鴨、上賀茂神社へ向かう。

Horse Race Event
(*kurabeuma-e-shinji*)

葵祭・競馬会神事
北区・上賀茂神社

In one of the events during the Aoi Fesitval at Kamigamo Shrine, two teams of horses and riders dressed in ceremonial robes compete in pre-matched pairings. The two-horse races date back to the 8th century.

5月5日、葵祭の前儀。

Festivals
京の祭

Dance of the Demons
(*Tsuinashiki Oni no Horaku*)

追儺式鬼法楽　上京区・廬山寺

Dancing demons are exorcised in the annual re-enactment of an ancient court practice on February 3rd (*setsubun*) at Rozan-ji Temple, the home of Heian author Murasaki Shikibu.

紫式部ゆかりの寺。鬼法楽は2月3日の節分行事。

Festival of the Ages
(*Jidai Matsuri*)

時代祭　左京区・岡崎

On October 22nd every year, the splendor of Kyoto through the ages comes to life from the Meiji Era (1868-1912) back to the Heian Period (794-1185). The two-hour procession starts at the Imperial Palace headed for Heian Jingu Shrine.

10月22日、京都御所を出発して平安神宮へ。

洛西 Kyoto West

Tenryu-ji Temple

The conflict between the Emperor Go-Daigo (Southern Court) and Shogun Ashikaga Takauji (Northern Court) during the Namboku-cho Period finally came to an end in the late 14th century. The monk Muso Soseki convinced Takauji to build a memorial for those who perished in war, but there were no funds. So ships (*Tenryu-ji bune*) were sent to China as trade missions to raise money to build Tenryu-ji. Soseki was a gifted landscaper who "borrowed" background views of the Arashiyama Mountains for the garden's backdrop, and his style became the benchmark in Japanese garden design. Tenryu-ji repeated a cycle of fire damage and reconstruction. When the Imperial loyalists rebelled against the Tokugawa Shogunate (Kinmon Incident, 1864), it was left in such a ruinous state that restoration was even thought to be hopeless. A path through the dim bamboo grove at the north gate of the temple exposes a fabulous viewpoint of the entire city of Kyoto from the former estate of samurai movie actor Okochi Denjiro.

天龍寺　世界遺産　禅宗　　　　　　　　　　　　　　　　　　右京区・嵯峨天龍寺

　南北朝の争乱期、後醍醐天皇と足利尊氏の激しい戦がようやく統一された（14世紀末）。天皇と両軍の戦死者の菩提を弔うため、安国寺と利生塔を建てるよう夢窓疎石が尊氏に進言する。天龍寺の始まりだが造営費が不足。天竜寺船を元に派遣して莫大な利益を得て建造は進んだ。疎石は秀でた造園家。背後の嵐山を借景とした壮大な庭園を天龍寺に築き、後世の範となった。応仁の乱で荒廃、幕末には"蛤御門の変"で長州藩が拠点とした寺を薩摩藩が焼討ちして再建不能とまで思われた。寺の北門の仄暗い竹林の道を辿ると大河内山荘。昭和初期の時代劇の大スター・大河内伝次郎が造り上げた広大な山荘。京都市街が一望出来る。

Togetsu-kyo Bridge

The Moon Crossing Bridge (*Togetsu-kyo*) is a landmark. Heian Court nobles floated their boats on the Oi River, enjoying elaborate parties on the water with poetry, song and music. Many poems were written by Heian poets. Arashiyama's cherry trees were brought in from Yoshino and planted during the Kamakura Period. In the fall, the entire hillside turns into a glorious display of fall colors. Crowds flock to enjoy the spectacular sight from the shoreline, from the bridge, and from boats. Downstream from the bridge is Katsura River. Children turning thirteen years old visit Horin-ji Temple on the southern shore to pray for wisdom (*Jusan Mairi*). Dressed in formal attire, they cannot look back on their way home or they might drop the wisdom they just received. They look so sweet as they walk straight ahead with determination! Posh restaurants can be found on the river banks, along with many shops that serve *yudofu*. The scenic environment is perfect for viewing the leaves turning colors over an excellent meal.

嵐山渡月橋

西京区・嵐山

　"満月の渡るに似る"と評された渡月橋は嵐山のシンボル。平安期には公貴族が大堰川(おおいがわ)で船遊びを楽しみ多くの歌人が和歌に詠んだ。春と秋には詩、歌、管弦の三船を浮かべ優雅な芸能を繰り広げるのはその名残りである。鎌倉期に吉野の桜を移植して桜の名所にもなった。秋には嵐山全山が紅葉するのだから壮観だ。岸辺から橋上、船から紅葉を楽しむ人達で嵐山は大変な混雑となる。橋から下流は桂川となる。南岸の法輪寺は十三詣で知られる。虚空蔵に知恵を授けてもらい、帰途に後を振り返ると知恵を落とすという。懸命に前を睨んで歩く着物姿の子ども達はほほえましい。川岸には高級料亭、旅館が並び、湯豆腐の店も多い。紅葉に酔いしれ、美食を楽しむのもこの景観のおかげである。

嵯峨竹林 右京区・嵯峨

JR、嵐電嵐山駅から竹林の道を辿る。小さな野宮神社、天龍寺北門、落柿舎にかけて竹林が広がる。仄暗い竹林の中、陽が射し込み葉に反射する光は躍るよう。風はサヤサヤと幽かな音を残して過ぎ去る。光と陰の妙が人々を魅了する。枯れ枝を束ねた笹穂垣の小径はうねりつつ奥の迷宮へ誘うかのよう。世に無常を感じた人達は都から遠く寂しい嵯峨野に隠棲した。清盛に邸を追われた白拍子が結んだ庵が祇王寺。その隣は滝口寺。北面の武士が建礼門院の雑仕女に恋をするも親の反対で絶望、出家して滝口入道となった。それを知った横笛は寺を探して事情を弁明するも出家の身には届かない。滝口は高野山へ。横笛は出家して奈良の法華寺へ。また大堰川の千鳥ヶ淵に身を投げたとも。

Saga Bamboo Forest

From Arashiyama train station, the path through the bamboo forest spreads out toward the small Nonomiya Shrine, to the north gate of Tenryu-ji Temple and to Rakushisha. Sunlight streams through the tall stalks of bamboo, dropping fragments of light to dance on the leaves, while a gentle breeze leaves behind a faint murmur. The play of light and shadow is enchanting. The fence made of dried bamboo branches hug the path as it continues through twists and turns, pushing deeper into a maze. Being isolated in Sagano was ideal for those who sensed impermanence and sought a reclusive life far from the capital. The jilted mistress of Taira Kiyomori was one such recluse who entered the nunnery at Gio-ji Temple (see P47). Takiguchi was another, for whom the temple next door is named. He was a nobleman soldier whose father forbade him to marry his love (*Yokobue*). Despaired, he entered priesthood. Yokobue followed and beseeched him at the temple, but he desisted and moved to Mt. Koya. Yokobue then took vows as a nun and entered Hokke-ji Temple in Nara, although according to some accounts, she threw herself into the Oi River.

Gio-ji Temple

In the first chapter of *The Tales of the Heike*, the Story of the Lady Gio referred to Kiyomori's arrogance and contempt. The story recounted a beautiful 19-year-old dancer (*Gio*) who was favored by Kiyomori. One day, another dancer (*Hotoke*) from the Kaga Province requested an audience with Kiyomori but he turned her away. Gio kindly interceded, giving Hotoke a chance to perform. Kiyomori became smitten by Hotoke and dismissed Gio, her sister and mother from his estate. The women secluded themselves in Sagano as nuns. Later, the remorseful Hotoke joined them to live in peaceful prayer. Where Sagano dead-ends at Mt.Ogura and Western Paradise (*Saiho Jodo*) lies beyond, colorful autumn leaves shine like lights from another world. Next to Gio-ji, Danrin-ji is the temple of the Empress to the Emperor Saga. At Nison-in Temple a little south of Gio-ji, maples and cherry trees form a single track beyond the entry gate. The statues of *Shaka Nyorai* (who welcomes life) and *Amida Nyorai* (who welcomes the afterlife) are said to provide comfort.

祇王寺　　　真言宗　　　　　　　　　　　　　　　　　　　　　　　　　　　　右京区・嵯峨鳥居本

　世のそしりも嘲笑も憚らない清盛の行いが『平家物語』の祇王に語られる。19歳の白拍子はその美貌と気品のある舞が気に入られ、清盛に寵愛された。ある日、加賀の仏御前が清盛の邸を訪ねるが門前払いとなる。祇王の心遣いで清盛の前で舞うことが出来た。清盛はすっかり虜となり、母妹と共に邸を追われる。三人は出家して嵯峨野に隠棲。その後、仏御前が庵を訪ね、自らの行いを悔いて共に念仏三昧の日々を送った。嵯峨野は小倉山に遮られて行き止まりだが、その彼方は西方浄土。鮮やかな紅葉は浄土の灯りのようだ。すぐ隣は嵯峨天皇の皇后の檀林寺。少し南が二尊院。風格のある門から一直線の"紅葉の馬場"は桜と楓が並ぶ。釈迦如来と阿弥陀の二尊が祀られ、現世と来世の安らぎが得られるという。

Rakushisha

Where the path in the dim bamboo grove comes to an end, the farm fields at the base of Mt. Ogura open wide. Mt. Atago (924 m) is visible to the north. On the other side of the farm fields, the Villa of the Fallen Persimmons (*Rakushisha*) is a cottage where one of master poet Matsuo Basho's ten disciples, Mukai Kyorai, ran a haiku school for anyone interested in poetry. A sign posted in the tiny hut warned group nappers not to snore. Basho wrote about his fond visits to the mild clime of Sagano in *Saga Diary* after he returned from the harsh environment of northern Japan. Jojakko-ji Temple has a simple thatched roof on the Niomon Gate. Just south of the cottage and a popular spot for fall foliage, it blends into the countryside without a fence. Sei Shonagon wrote about Mt. Ogura in *The Pillow Book*, while the Heian poet laureate Fujiwara Teika compiled the one hundred poems by one hundred poets at his villa. Near Nison-in Temple is a shop specializing in home-made tofu, a regional favorite.

落柿舎 右京区・嵯峨小倉山

　仄暗い竹林の道を抜けると小倉山々麓に田畑が広がる。北には火伏せの神・愛宕山(924m)が見える。畑の向こうの小さな茅葺屋根が落柿舎。蕉門十哲の一人、向井去来が開いた俳諧道場は誰でも出入は自由。狭い古屋で雑魚寝する人達に"大鼾かくべからず"の貼り紙がある。厳しい自然の奥州から戻った芭蕉は穏やかな嵯峨野を気に入り四度も訪れ『嵯峨日記』を著した。すぐ南の常寂光寺は塀もなく、里山に融け込んでいる。素朴な茅葺の仁王門がとても良い。紅葉の名所。「山は をぐらやま」（枕草子）。藤原定家は山荘を設け小倉百人一首を編んだ。寺の北、二尊院のすぐ近くの厭離庵には定家塚があるが後世のもの。この近くに美味しい豆腐屋がある。嵯峨豆腐は古くから親しまれてきた。

Adashino Nenbutsu-ji Temple

Just before the Ichino Torii gate at Atago Shrine, there are an overwhelming number of steps to climb. There are thousands of steps. Kukai established Nenbutsu-ji Temple to mourn the souls of the deceased; then Honen took over the temple. The area was a necropolis in ancient times. As Buddhist monk and author Yoshida Kenko described the place: "If man were never to fade away like the dew of Adashino," in this world, impermanence would be imminent (see P64). In August, a candlelight memorial service (*sento kuyo*) takes place in remembrance of the deceased who were left here. By dusk, the quivering flames of the candles create a mystical aura. At the Seiryo-ji Temple a kilometer away southeast, the Saga Dainenbutsu Kyogen performed every April has a history of 700 years. It is one of the three major silent Buddhist plays (*nenbutstu kyogen*) of Kyoto. The temple is especially crowded on the day of the performance since one of the three major fire festivals (*Saga Otaimatsu-shiki*) is also held on the same day to forecast the year's harvest.

化野念仏寺　　浄土宗　　　　　　　　　　　　　　　　　　　　　　右京区・嵯峨鳥居本

　愛宕山一之鳥居の少し手前の石段を上る。数千という石塔の列には驚かされる。古来、この辺りは風葬の地であった。空海が死者の菩提を弔う霊場とし、法然上人が受け継いだ。兼好法師が「あだし野の露、消ゆる時なく」と述べた地。人の世の無常が迫る。8月の千灯供養は夕闇に揺れるローソクの灯りで幻想的な空気に包まれる。寺から南東1kmほどの清凉寺では4月、700年の歴史がある嵯峨大念仏狂言が催される。壬生、千本ゑんま堂の三大念仏狂言の一つ。同じ日、嵯峨お松明で寺は人で溢れる。鞍馬の火祭、五山送り火の京都三大火祭の一つ。作物の豊凶を占う行事である。

Saga Toriimoto

On the other side of Adashino Nenbutsu-ji Temple, Saga Toriimoto is at the far end of Kyoto. Old farm houses with thatched roofs dating back to the Edo period are part of the preservation district. The large crimson Ichino Torii Gate belongs to Atago Shrine. The god enshrined here protects Kyoto from fire. Right next to the *torii* gate is a teahouse that has been serving sweetfish since early Edo period, still very popular. Its large paper lantern, antiquated curtain and red carpet have dramatic style. There is a tunnel just inside the *torii* that leads to Kiyotaka River. The 5 km uphill hike after the Toen-kyo Bridge is not an easy climb. Ascetic practitioners gathered at Atago Shrine during the Kamakura Period. Akechi Mitsuhide prayed to the *shogun jizo* before heading off to Honno-ji Temple to assassinate Oda Nobunaga. In the summer, throngs of people head for the mountain top to pray for blessings that would last a thousand days during the festival of *Sen-nichi Mairi*. A downhill path going south leads to Mizuo, where the Japanese citrus fruit *yuzu* are grown. Between a *yuzu* hot bath and a chicken hot pot, what better way to finish off a good hike?

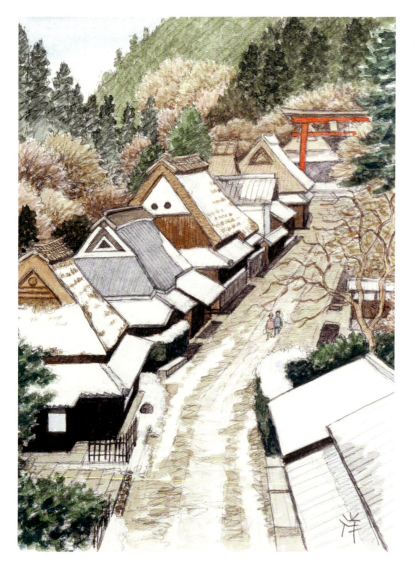

嵯峨鳥居本

伝統的建造物群保存地区

右京区・嵯峨鳥居本

化野念仏寺を過ぎると、もう京洛の最果ての地。江戸期からの古い茅葺の農家、民家が残っている。朱塗りの大きな鳥居は火伏せの神・愛宕神社一之鳥居。その脇に江戸初期からという鮎茶屋は今も人気の店。大きな提灯、古い暖簾、赤い毛氈が印象的。江戸末期に愛宕詣が盛んとなり、門前町として発展した。鳥居からすぐ西のトンネルを抜けると清滝川。渡猿橋を渡り5kmほどの急坂の参道はかなりきつい。愛宕神社は鎌倉頃から修験者が集まってきた。明智光秀は社の勝軍地蔵に祈願して、向かった先は本能寺。夏の"千日詣"には各地から大勢の人々が山上を目指す。参道の途中、南へ降りる道を辿ると柚の里・水尾。柚子風呂と鶏の水炊きが名物。登山の汗を流すには最高だ。

Sagano in Spring

It is peaceful in the countryside of northern Saga, where farm fields stretch out lazily. And so it has been since the time Sei Shonagon wrote about Sagano in *The Pillow Book*. Blooms of yellow rapes, lotuses, daisies, and cherry trees abound in spring. New sprouts on the willows and the pampas grasses by the water's edge glisten in the sun, letting the breezes flow through the reeds. After the harvest and once the leaves have dropped, Sagano's landscape changes to a drab ink painting (*sumi-e*). The road from city center to the Emperor Saga's former palace (Saga-in, now Daikaku-ji Temple) has been mentioned in so many poems. Hirosawa and Osawa Ponds are like paradise to water birds, keeping photographers busy trying to capture them in frames. Both ponds are still favorite moon-viewing spots. Near the Ominato train station south of Sagano, Koryu-ji Temple houses a statue of the *Miroku Bosatsu* with a refreshingly archaic smile. Since movie studios are nearby, with any luck you might even run into a celebrity. Film set tours, ninja shows and sword fights are among some of the events that visitors can enjoy at the Toei Studio Park (*Toei Eigamura*).

嵯峨野の春

右京区・嵯峨広沢

「野は 嵯峨野 さらなり」（枕草子）。北嵯峨は田畑が広がり長閑だ。春は菜の花、れんげ、たんぽぽ、桜が咲く。池畔の柳、葦の若葉は陽光に輝き、そよ風が渡る。広沢、大沢池は観月の名所、そして水鳥の天国。カメラマンは鳥を追うのに忙しい。稲刈りが終わり紅葉が過ぎると嵯峨野は墨絵のような情景へと移ろう。都の中心部から嵯峨院へ向かう"千代の古道"は和歌によく詠まれてきた。嵯峨野の南、JR太秦駅近くに聖徳太子建立の広隆寺がある。寺の弥勒菩薩像のアルカイックスマイルは清々しい。近くに東映撮影所があり、運が良ければスターに出会えるかも。映画村では映画、テレビのセット、チャンバラショーが楽しみだ。

Daikaku-ji Temple Osawa Pond

Moving the capital was not a straightforward task for the Emperor Kanmu, whose fear of haunting spirits affected the transition. Matters finally stabilized when the Emperor Saga ascended to the throne, developed Sagano and built the Saga-in imperial villa as the forerunner to Daikaku-ji. Poetry contests and great parties were held, and the monk Kukai told stories of China from his experiences there. Osawa Pond was built in the likeness of Dong Ting Lake, on which boats with heads of the dragon (*ryutosen*) and Chinese heron (*gekishusen*) at the bow were floated. More like a small scale imperial villa than a temple, Daikaku-ji houses lustrous paintings on interior sliding doors (*fusuma-e*) done by Kano Sanraku that transfix the eye. Jikishian Temple is to the north. Hirosawa Pond appears as a large body of water up close to the east. At Seiryo-ji Temple to the south, the standing statue of *Shaka Nyorai* introduced from China's Sung Dynasty has been the subject of devotion among the masses. This is the land where prominent Court official, poet and prince of the Emperor Saga, Minamoto no Toru, kept a mountain villa. He is believed to be the model for the main character in *The Tale of Genji*.

大覚寺・大沢池　　　真言宗　　　　　　　　　　　　　　　　　　　右京区・嵯峨大沢町

　平安京遷都で桓武天皇は怨霊におびえ、迷走しながら建都は進んだ。嵯峨天皇の代にようやく安定期を迎える。嵯峨野を開発して離宮・嵯峨院を営んだのが寺の前身である。歌会、宴を催し、長安帰りの空海を招いて唐の文化を知る。広い大沢池は唐の洞庭湖を模して龍頭、鷁首舟を浮かべて観月を楽しんだ。大覚寺は寺というより小御所ともいえる王朝文化の高貴な佇まいである。狩野山楽の艶やかな襖絵には目を見張る。寺の北には直指庵。東の広大な広沢池も間近に見える。南の清涼寺には宋伝来の釈迦如来立像が庶民の信仰を集めてきた。嵯峨天皇の皇子・源融が山荘を営んだ地である。融は左大臣にまで昇り詰め、源氏物語のモデルともいわれる。

Jingo-ji Temple

The stone steps going downhill from the Takao bus stop on Shuzan Kaido last forever, then a steep uphill climb after crossing the Kiyotaki River finally reaches the gate to Jingo-ji. The temple's founder, Wake no Kiyomaru, suggested Kyoto as a potential site to the Emperor Kanmu, who was challenged by the relocation of the capital. Jingo-ji was turned into a school for esoteric Shingon Buddhism upon Kukai's return from China, but the buildings were later destroyed. The warrior monk Mongaku demanded donations from the Emperor Go-Shirakawa to refurbish the temple, was exiled to Kanto and wasted no time in persuading Minamoto Yoritomo to overthrow the Heike. Under Shogun Yoritomo's patronage, the temple was reconstructed flawlessly. Yoritomo's portrait is one of the temple's treasures. Directly north, the Kozan-ji Temple displays illustrations (*Choju jinbutsu giga*) that inspired *manga* comic books. These humorous originals portray life for the poverty-stricken commoners of the late Heian Period.

神護寺　　　真言宗　　　　　　　　　　　　　　　　　　　　　　　右京区・梅ヶ畑高雄

　周山街道の高雄バス停から急な石段を延々と降りる。清滝川を渡り急な石段を喘ぎながら上るとやっと寺の山門。遷都に苦悩する桓武天皇に、山城の地を勧めた和気清麻呂が発願したのが神護寺。唐から戻った空海が真言密教の道場としたが、その後に荒廃した。荒法師・文覚上人が後白河法皇に再興の費用を強要して関東へ流罪となる。彼はすぐさま頼朝に会って平家打倒を進言する。将軍となった頼朝の援助で寺は見事に再興した。頼朝画像は寺宝である。すぐ北に高山寺が建つ。名僧・明恵上人は孤高の人。多くの人に慕われた。寺は漫画のルーツ『鳥獣人物戯画巻』を所蔵する。ユーモラスな風刺画には平安末期、貧困に苦しんだ庶民の逞しい息吹が脈打っている。

保津川下り

右京区・嵯峨

　京洛の北は丹波の山並みが若狭湾まで続く。その山塊から発した保津川は16kmの保津峡を下って嵐山に至る。保津峡は急流、川底が浅い所が多く船運には不適だった。豪商の角倉了以は岩を砕き、川底を掘り下げ、河川で使う高瀬舟を浮かべた。丹波の木材、薪炭、農産物の船運を独占して莫大な利益を上げた。山陰道の老ノ坂峠を越えた馬借は失業となった。水しぶきを浴びる川下りに観光客は大はしゃぎ。川下りにはJR嵯峨嵐山駅でトロッコ列車に乗るのが便利。保津川沿いに走るトロッコは桜や紅葉の名所でもある。この列車を最も喜ぶのは遠足の子ども達。その黄色い歓声は谷にこだまして賑やかだ。

Hozu River boat ride

The mountains of Tanba stretch all the way from the north of Kyoto to Wakasa Bay. The Hozu River runs from this mountain range for 16 km into Arashiyama. It is a rapid strait that was very shallow in many places, making it hard for boats to maneuver through before shipping magnate Suminokura Ryoi dredged the river bottom so his canal boats (*takasebune*) could have access to the Tanba region. He monopolized the transport of lumber, charcoal and produce to Kyoto, putting horse-packers crossing the Oinosaka Pass (*Oinosaka Toge*) on the Sanin Road (*Sanindo*) out of business. Getting wet from the water spray will not stop tourists on the downstream boat ride from having a great time. The locomotive (*torokko*) from Arashiyama train station is convenient to the boarding site. The scenic ride along the river is fabulous when cherry blossoms and autumn maples are in season. Children might enjoy the train ride the most, letting their excited voices echo in the gorge.

Katsura Imperial Villa

Katsura-dono and Katsura-ya were both located between Arashiyama and the Katsura River; the former being the fictitious villa of *The Tale of Genji* hero Hikaru Genji, and the latter being statesman Fujiwara Michinaga's villa. The area is also a fine place for gazing at the moon. When the Tokugawa government (*Bakufu*) prohibited members of the imperial household from engaging in political activity, Emperor Go-Mizuno-o began construction of Shugakuin Imperial Villa, while his uncle, the Prince Hachijo Toshihito, began construction of Katsura Imperial Villa. These villas were designed to be the very essence of court culture in tacit rebellion against the *Bakufu* (see P65). A little upstream is Matsuno-o Taisha, an old shrine that has served to protect Capital West. Its natural spring is said to be blessed for sake. South of the shrine, Saijo-ji Temple is commonly known as Koke Dera for the moss garden that shrouds the temple in ethereal beauty.

桂離宮　　　　　　　　　　　　　　　　　　　　　　　　　　　　　　西京区・桂

　嵐山から桂川の流域は光源氏が桂殿、藤原道長が桂家という別荘を営んだ地。そして月の名所である。徳川幕府が「禁中並公家諸法度」を公布、政治活動の禁止である。後水尾上皇は修学院離宮、叔父の八条宮智仁親王は桂離宮の造営を始める。王朝文化の神髄ともいえる離宮、文化力という幕府への静かな反抗である。桂川の水を引き入れ、壮大な回遊式庭園は随所に様々な仕掛を施し、茶室、東屋そして雁行形に並ぶ高床式の書院は風雅そのもの。建築家ブルーノ・タウトが「永遠なるもの」と激賞したほどだ。少し上流の松尾大社は秦氏が営んだ洛西鎮護の古社。そして名水が湧き、酒の神と崇敬されてきた。社の南の苔寺は境内一面が苔に覆われた幽玄な世界である。

洛南 Kyoto South

Fushimi Inari-taisha Shrine

At the southern edge of Higashiyama Sanjuroppo is Mt. Inari, the southern peak upon which the gods descended. Here, the Hata clan enshrined a diety of agriculture, and the fox became a symbolic messenger of god. Fushimi Inari-taisha is the head of more than 40,000 *inari* shrines throughout Japan. Twin tunnels of over a thousand bright crimson-colored *torii* gates are dazzling (see P65). An astounding number of people come to pray for a bountiful harvest, for prosperous business, for safety, even for a good match. Once past the *torii* gate just outside Inari train station, the main path to the shrine is crowded with shops selling a variety of foods and wares. Farmers believed that the soil from Mt. Inari mixed into the field would yield bountiful crops. The Fushimi Doll was the first clay doll in Japan. Images of foxes, children, gadgets, chicks and animals are cute and colorful.

伏見稲荷神社参道

伏見区・深草

　東山三十六峰の南端が稲荷山。神が降臨する神南備山として古くから信仰された。秦氏が農耕神を祀ったのが稲荷信仰となり、狐は神の使いである。全国に４万社ともいう稲荷社の総本宮は朱の色で目がくらみそう。二列のトンネル状の千本鳥居には驚かされる。五穀豊穣から商売繁盛、厄除け、縁結びと現世利益を願い参拝する人の数は凄い。稲荷駅から鳥居をくぐると参道には神具から稲荷寿司、うどん、焼鳥、土産物の店がカラフルに続いている。稲荷山の土を田畑に撒くと豊作になると信じられた。その土で作った伏見人形は日本で最も古い土人形。狐は勿論、饅頭食い、子ども、道真、雛、動物などユーモラスでカラフルだ。

Canal Along Fushimi Sake District

When Hideyoshi built Fushimi Castle, he redirected part of the Uji River to surround it with a moat in the middle of town. He also built a port, so that a canal could run through Kyoto from Osaka to Edo. Fushimi was blessed with natural groundwater. It was also a rice cradle that developed into a booming sake industry by the beginning of the Edo period. But government policy helped the less expensive sake from Omi Province into broader distribution, and all but two breweries were driven out of business. Fushimi's sake production revived once rail transportation provided better access to Kanto in the Meiji era. While Nada produces a dry, masculine sake from hard water, Fushimi's soft water creates a sweeter, more feminine sake. Old storehouses can still be spotted throughout the town. Just west of the brewery, Sakamoto Ryoma stayed on a regular basis at the Teradaya inn. During the Battle of Toba-Fushimi (1868), the Satsuma forces confronted the Shogun's army in Fushimi. Gokonomiya Shrine was built upon a medicinal spring.

伏見酒蔵と運河

伏見区・南浜町

　秀吉は伏見城を築き、宇治川の水を利用して町中に堀割を廻らして港を築いた。京の都は大阪から江戸への水運が可能となった。伏見は伏流水が豊かで米所でもあった。名水と米で酒造が始まり、奉行の奨励で江戸初期に最盛となった。しかし幕府の統制があり近江の安い酒が広がって衰退。細々と２軒だけが残った。明治になり鉄道が開通すると関東への販路を広げて見事に復活した。灘は硬水で辛口の男酒、伏見は軟水で甘口の女酒と評される。保温に適した重厚な酒蔵が町のあちらこちらに連なっている。この酒蔵のすぐ西に坂本龍馬が常宿とした船宿・寺田屋が残る。御香宮神社は病人でも治る聖水が湧いたことで始まった。鳥羽・伏見の戦では薩摩軍が社に陣を構え、奉行所の幕府軍と対峙した。

Daigo-ji Temple

A 90-minute drive on the mountain road from Biwa is Kamidaigo, where Rigen Daishi established a small abbey in the latter half of the 9th century. Several structures were built within the Daigo-ji compound once it became the Emperor Daigo's official temple. More structures were added under the patronage of the Ashikaga shoguns during the Muromachi Period, followed by a major restoration project by Toyotomi Hideyoshi (see P65). To the North, Zuishin-in Temple was where Ono no Komachi, the legendary Heian Court beauty and accomplished poet, took refuge to quietly fade in her aging years. To the South, Hokai-ji Temple (also known as Hino Yakushi) was converted to a temple from a villa of the Hino family, relations to the powerful Fujiwara. Among the Hino family members were Shin Buddhism founder Shinran and Hino Tomiko, mother of ninth Ashikaga shogun Yoshihisa.

醍醐寺・桜の馬場　世界遺産　真言宗　　　　　　　　　　　　　　　　　　伏見区・醍醐

　麓から1時間半もの山道を登った上醍醐に理源大師が小堂を開いたのが9世紀後半。開山堂、如意輪堂、五大力堂などが連なる。醍醐天皇の勅願寺となり発展した。そして下醍醐の建設も進む。室町時代に足利将軍の帰依で全盛となるが応仁の乱で焼失、衰退した。これを再興したのが秀吉。傾いた五重塔、塔頭を土木建築の技術集団が修復、再建した。そして近江、河内、大和、山城から700本の桜を移植して"醍醐の花見"を催す。朝鮮出兵の失敗、幼い秀頼と自らの老いを感じ最後の豪遊である。5ヵ月後に死去、そして豊臣氏は滅亡。すぐ北には小野小町ゆかりの随心院がある。南には日野薬師で知られる法界寺がある。親鸞聖人生誕の地、日野富子の出身地である。

Byodo-in Temple

Nature is picturesque under a draping mist along the Uji River as it flows downstream from Lake Biwa. Heian court nobles built villas here to amuse themselves with poetry and music. The idyllic setting appeared in period literature ranging from an 8th century poetry collection to the first work of fiction to religious writings. The splendor of Japanese Court culture peaked under Fujiwara Michinaga, Regent to the Emperor. Son Michiyori, also Regent, built Byodo-in Temple designed to look like a phoenix spreading its wings in flight. The statue of *Amida Nyorai* was placed inside, and the interior was painted in elaborate patterns and intense colors (see P65). Also in Uji, Manpuku-ji Temple is the head of the Obaku Zen sect and is well known for serving a type of Zen cuisine called Fucha Ryori. Mimuroto-ji Temple is the 10th of the 33 pilgrimage temples (*Saigoku Kannon Reijo*). Known as the flower temple, it bursts with blooms of the lotus flower, azaleas, and hydrangeas in spring.

平等院 世界遺産 宇治市・宇治

　琵琶湖から流れ下った宇治川は桜、紅葉、清流と川霧が美しい。貴族達は別荘を建て詩歌管弦の宴を繰り広げた。万葉集にも歌われ、源氏物語の舞台となった地。「極楽いぶかしくば宇治の御寺をうやまへ」（後拾遺往生伝）。平等院は鳳凰が翼を広げ、まるで飛んでいるような建築。王朝文化が華やぐ世は末法の時代と信じられた。貴族達はひたすら阿弥陀仏に祈り極楽浄土への往生を願った。栄華を極めた藤原道長の子、関白頼通は平等院を建て、阿弥陀如来（定朝作）を安置、堂内は極彩色の文様を描き現世の極楽浄土を出現させ、往生を願った。院の北方3km、普茶料理で知られる黄檗宗・萬福寺は中国へ来たのかと錯覚する。西国観音霊場の第十番札所・三室戸寺は花の寺。蓮、つつじ、紫陽花が咲き乱れる。

Tea Fields of Uji

Uji was a region that was under Tokugawa government control. Tea was purveyed to the Shogun in Edo via special "tea pot journeys," the sighting of which made its way into a nursery rhyme. In the Kamakura Period, Kennin-ji founder Eisai brought back tea from China. He shared the seeds with the High Priest Myoe of Kozan-ji, and Myoe expanded tea cultivation near Manpuku-ji. That started Uji tea. Rikyu and many tea masters popularized the art of tea ceremony at Daitoku-ji. In recent years, residential development has encroached upon tea fields in Uji City. At the southern end of Ujitawara, though, rows and rows of neatly planted bushes still look as if mosaic tiles were skillfully placed one by one. Before Nagatani Soen discovered a breakthrough method to process tea leaves en masse, green tea was a luxury reserved for the privileged. Among the once dozens of tea makers, only Kanbayashi Shunsho remains in operation today. Merchants in business for generations line the path from Uji train station, filling the air with the gentle aroma of tea.

宇治茶の郷

京都府綴喜郡・宇治田原町

　「茶壺に追われてとっぴんしゃん」。宇治は徳川幕府の直轄地となる。ここで茶師が製造した茶は"茶壺道中"で江戸に献上された。鎌倉期に建仁寺の開祖・栄西禅師が中国から茶を持ち帰り、高山寺の明恵上人に種を贈る。上人は萬福寺の近くで茶の栽培を広めた。茶づらの大徳寺で利休や多くの茶人が茶の湯を広めた。宇治市は宅地が広がり茶畑は少なくなった。南の宇治田原はなだらかな山並みに広がる茶畑は美しいモザイク模様。この地の永谷宗円が煎茶の製造法を確立して大衆に茶が広まった。JR宇治駅から平等院への参道には老舗の茶商が並び良い香りが漂う。古くは十数軒あった長屋門の茶師で上林記念館が唯一残った。

More information

Original Japanese titles of literary classics mentioned in this book:

The Tales of the Heike	*Heike Monogatari* various authors
The Pillow Book	*Makura no Soshi* by Sei Shonagon
Essays in Idleness	*Tsurezuregusa* by Yoshida Kenko
The Tale of Genji	*Genji Monogatari* by Murasaki Shikibu
Saga Diary	*Saga Nikki* by Matsuo Basho
A Hundred Poems by A Hundred Poets	*Ogura Hyakunin Isshu* compiled by Fujiwara Teika

⇨P10   Teramachi Gomon and Daimonji-yama

The monument marking the original palace is in a park near Senbon-maruta-machi west of where the Palace stands today. Kyoto was the seat of the Imperial throne, repeatedly caught in civil war as political factions and warlords fought for power. Ironically, these battles would burn down the splendid city, at times forcing an impoverished Court to move around to any available space. When the samurai warrior class came to rule, the aristocracy lost their positions of power but they continued to maintain residence around the Palace. In the 1860s, the same area would once again set stage for a historical turn of events. The Tokugawa Shogunate was displaced, the Edo Period ended, and Japan opened its doors to the rest of the world.

⇨P13   Kamogawa and Noryo yuka

The Emperor Shirakawa (1056-1129) used three examples for things one could not control in life: "There are but three things in my dominions that do not obey me: the water of the Kamo River, the dice of the sugoroku game, and the priests of Buddha." (Henry Cabot Lodge, The *History of Nations*, Volume 7, p. 55, 1916). The currents of the Kamo River raged out of control and flooded Heian-kyo often; the roll of a dice was a game of chance; and the warrior monks from Mt. Hiei would descend upon the city and wreak havoc upon the citizens.

⇨P14   Ponto-cho

Although *ochaya* is frequently translated as "teahouse" in English, it is not always the same as a tearoom where tea and coffee are served restaurant-style. Ochaya took on a new meaning as the merchant class became more affluent. Operating as exclusive establishments for private *geiko* entertainment, discretion and strict protocol are still keenly observed today. Many former ochaya have since converted to restaurants. The room dedicated for tea ceremonies, *cha shitsu*, were usually detached structures in the garden when space allowed, or they could be built inside the residence. *Cha shitsu* are designed for function, for aesthetic pleasure and for intellectual stimulation through both conversation and in silence.

⇨P16 Nijo Castle Higashi Otemon Gate

Nijo Castle once boasted a five-story tower, Tenmonkaku, that was later lost to a lightning strike. The Emperor Go Mizuno-o was an unwilling houseguest at the invitation of third shogun Iemitsu, who intended the Imperial visit to show the Emperor's tacit submission to samurai rule. And Iemitsu's command of 300,000 troops at Nijo Castle ensured that the Tokugawa power reverberated throughout the land. As the new government in Edo became stable, the successive shoguns no longer had a use for the castle and its glory was forgotten.

⇨P17 Kitano Tenmangu Shrine

Kitano was a desolate area northwest of Heian-kyo where there was a simple shrine dedicated to the gods of agriculture. Since the Sugawara family was deeply entwined with these gods, Kitano seemed a befitting site to build a shrine for Michizane. Kami-shichi-ken originated as a single teahouse built from scraps when the Tenmangu Shrine was reconstructed in 1607. An entire neighborhood grew, frequented by gentlemen clients who were predominantly silk merchants from the nearby Nishijin textile district.

⇨P18 Daitoku-ji Temple

Hunting parties years ago held outdoor tea socials (*nodate*) by simpifying the tea ceremony for the field. Today, an informally whisked bowl of tea, good conversation and natural surroundings can still be a pleasant way to relax.

⇨P24 Tofuku-ji Temple

East of Tofuku-ji is a secluded temple that is in a class of its own. Senyuji is a *miidera*, the mortuary temple for the Imperial family where 13 successive emperors are entombed in the Imperial mausoleum. The grounds were closed to the general public for 700 years until the 1950s. The downhill path from the main gate leads to some of the most ethereal buildings in a basin surrounded by hills.

⇨P29 Kyoto Minamiza Theatre

Maiko follow strict tradition and stringent codes of professional conduct. They train for years to become accomplished in Japanese dance, musical instruments such as *shamisen* and *koto*, learn the tea ceremony and other arts before they are ready to perform at a banquet. To complement the elaborate kimono dress, *maiko* wear fancy combs and ornaments in their hair done in the Japanese style, and tall wooden *pokkuri* on their feet that make gentle *klok klok* sounds as they hurry down the streets of Gion between lessons. White facial powder is applied carefully to pronounce their youthful beauty. Some day they might be called to a banquent at Ichiriki Teahouse, Kyoto's most exclusive establishment located on Gion's most famous street, Hanamikoji. Significant historical events have been discussed, planned, and carried out here.

⇨P32 Nanzen-ji Temple

Passing right through the temple grounds is a Roman aqueduct carrying water from Lake Biwa. Strangely it blends into the landscape. Nanzen-ji has its own natural spring, too, and the tofu hot pot is said to be the best ever since the Edo era.

⇨P36   Mt. Hiei
Under the patronage of the aristocracy, the compound at Enryaku-ji was expanded and priests were also trained as security forces. But the warrior monks grew violent and caused grave concern for the Emperor Shirakawa. All of Mt. Hiei is considered a seminary for the priests who take part in the spartan Thousand Day Walk (*Sennichi Kaihogyo*). Honen, Eisai, Shinran, Dogen and Nichiren all trained on Mt. Hiei before establishing their respective sects.

⇨P49   Adashino Nenbutsu-ji Temple
The translated line from Yoshida Kenko's description of Adashino is quoted from George Bailey Sansom's *The Tsuredzure Gusa of Yoshida No Kaneyoshi, Being the Meditations of a Recluse in the 14th Century* (1911).

⇨P55   Katsura Imperial Villa
German modernist architect Bruno Taut praised the imperial villa with the famous words, "Japan's architectural arts could not rise higher than Katsura." Indeed, the villa boasts some of the most outstanding examples of Japanese architecture from the period (1600s). No design element was spared: channeling in water from the Katsura River; strolling gardens with pleasant surprise features; multiple tea houses; garden structures (*azumaya*); raised floors; floor boards laid in an offset flying geese pattern.

⇨P56   Fushimi Inari-taisha Shrine
Fushimi Inari-taisha is famous for its network of red-lacquered *torii* gates that number in the thousands. Following them up the mountain can be a long hike through nature trails. Be prepared to spend a few hours enjoying some of the best views over Kyoto while sampling traditional treats from food stands along the way.

⇨P58   Daigo-ji Temple
Under Toyotomi Hideyoshi, a team of civil engineers righted the leaning five-story pagoda, and seven hundred cherry trees were imported from outlying areas for a grand scale party to view cherry blossoms. It was to be the last event that the elderly shogun shared with young son Hideyori. Hideyoshi passed away just five months later, and the Toyotomi line perished not long after.

⇨P59   Byodo-in Temple
Period literature described as an 8th century poetry collection was titled *Manyoshu*; the first Japanese work of fiction was *The Tale of Genji*; and religious writings were known as *Goshui Ojoden*. Pious aristocrats believed that their lavish lifestyle was slipping away in a period of declining Buddhism (*mappo* theory). They envisioned a Paradise (Pure Land) that was even more extravagant, and built the interior of Byodo-in in that image. They prayed fervently to the Amida Buddha seeking rebirth in the Pure Land.

Yohtaro Tsujimoto

Yohtaro Tsujimoto is a painter who lives in Kyoto. Born in 1942 in Nara, he graduated from Kyoto City University of Arts. Yohtaro has been commissioned for numerous storybook illustrations, and has also published collections of some of his sketches. *Manyo Travels, Manyo Travels II, Kyoto Leisurely Travel, Nara-Manyo Travels* are among his published works.

辻本洋太朗

1942 年奈良県生まれ。京都市立美術大学西洋画科（現 京都市立芸術大学）卒。

［著作］『万葉スケッチ紀行』『万葉スケッチ紀行 II』『京都のんびりスケッチ紀行』（淡交社）
『奈良 万葉スケッチ紀行』『放浪スケッチ紀行』（東方出版）

［絵本］『夢みるおすましやさん』（ふたば書房）『拝啓手紙です』（福音館書店）
『わたしはひろがる』（小峰書店）『12 しのおはなし』（メイト）

Stella Colucci

Born and raised in Tokyo, Stella attended Sophia University and later graduated from the University of Texas at Arlington (B.A., Political Science) and the University of Oklahoma (M.P.A.). As a translator, writer, former corporate executive and consultant, Stella has worked on various projects to promote relations between Japan and abroad. Her most recent publication is *Walking TOKYO*.

コルーチィ・ステラ

東京に生まれ育ち、上智大学国際学部で学んだ後、テキサス州立大学政治学部、オクラホマ大学大学院博士課程卒。
翻訳家、ライター、コンサルタントとして日米間を結ぶ様々なプロジェクトを手がける。近訳に『Walking TOKYO』。

編　集	木村由加子　金澤　隆
ブックデザイン	壁谷沢敦子
電子版制作	関根広告社
企画協力	山本美智代

Walking KYOTO 古都千年の彩譜

2016年1月27日　第1版第1刷発行
2016年2月 4日　第1版第2刷発行

著　者	辻本洋太朗
訳　者	コルーチィ・ステラ
発行者	木村由加子
発行所	まむかいブックスギャラリー
	〒108-0023　東京都港区芝浦3-14-19-6F
	TEL.050-3555-7335　www.mamukai.com

Paintings and text copyright ©2016 by Yohtaro Tsujimoto
Translation copyright ©2016 by Stella Colucci
Printed in Japan
ISBN 978-4-904402-05-4　C0095

＊落丁、乱丁本はお取り替え致します。
＊本書の一部あるいは全部を無断で複写複製することは法律で認められた場合を除き、著作権侵害となります。

Cutout

ねねの道 Nene-no-Michi ©Tomato Tsujimoto
Walking KYOTO www.mamukai.com/wk/

postcards

postcard

嵯峨竹林　Saga Bamboo Forest　©Yohtaro Tsujimoto
Walking KYOTO　www.mamukai.com/wk/

postcard

嵯峨鳥居本　Saga Toriimoto　©Yohtaro Tsujimoto
Walking KYOTO　www.mamukai.com/wk/

postcards

postcard

法然院　Honen-in Temple　©Yohtaro Tsujimoto
Walking KYOTO　www.mamukai.com/wk/

postcard

大原三千院・往生極楽院　Sanzen-in Temple　©Yohtaro Tsujimoto
Walking KYOTO　www.mamukai.com/wk/